Additional Praise for *Reviving the Congregation*

"Michael W. Foss is committed to the ministry of local congregations, convinced that this is the primary expression of the communion of saints. In *Reviving the Congregation*, he uses illustrations from his own experience in life and ministry to engage and encourage others who are called to lead. At a time when the contexts for ministry are rapidly changing, Pastor Mike Foss provides a welcome voice in the conversation about what it means to be the church, rooted in the gospel, and open to new ways of being faithful together."

Michael L. Burk
Bishop, Southeastern Iowa Synod, ELCA

"As a Lutheran Pastor who has worked with Pastor Foss, I can attest that his communication about first-century discipleship for the twenty-first century has always been concise, clear, and capturing. This book is one more example of this excellence."

Paul Borg
Pastor, ELCA

"Pastor Foss takes the challenges of pastoral leadership in the twenty-first century and addresses them in an honest, down-to-earth, practical way using concrete examples from his own ministry. A quick read with lasting impressions."

Suzanne Darcy Dillahunt
Bishop, Southern Ohio Synod, ELCA

"An important book for pastors and lay leaders alike! In a post-Christendom world, Foss focuses on first-century faith practices to transform lukewarm 'members' into passionate 'disciples.' In the process, he provides a helpful blueprint for the ministry of the local parish in the twenty-first century. In Foss, we meet an enthusiastic follower of Jesus sharing out of his abundant experience. The church will do well to listen."

Wolfgang D. Herz-Lane
Bishop, Delaware-Maryland Synod, ELCA

Reviving the Congregation

Reviving the Congregation

Pastoral Leadership in a Changing Context

Michael Foss

Fortress Press
Minneapolis

REVIVING THE CONGREGATION

Pastoral Leadership in a Changing Context

Cover design: Laurie Ingram

Cover images © blueenaylm/iStock/Thinkstock

Library of Congress Cataloging-in-Publication Data

Print ISBN: 978-1-4514-8288-1

eBook ISBN: 978-1-4514-8971-2

The paper used in this publication meets the minimum requirements of American National Standard for Information Sciences — Permanence of Paper for Printed Library Materials, ANSI Z329.48-1984.

Manufactured in the U.S.A.

This book was produced using PressBooks.com, and PDF rendering was done by PrinceXML.

Contents

1

Collision of Perspectives

The twenty-first century is an era of paradox for the local congregation. On the one hand, most homes in the United States have Bibles and revere them as the word of God. On the other hand, most adults in this country do not read the Bible. Most of them form their understanding of what the church believes through either the exaggerated exposés of the media or through limited personal experience. The spiritual hunger of our time is, I believe, great—but few adults identify the local congregation as a place where that hunger can be met in a spirit of acceptance and nurture. When the experience of the local church fits these two together, there is a combustion of the Spirit. Those who have experienced the welcome, acceptance, and nurture of their spiritual journey in a local church share it with their friends. This is the challenge and opportunity before us.

New-World Episodes

I met a couple in our New Member/Disciple Class and I assumed they had decided to join. I was surprised when, after the class, they shared they were just interested in learning more about our church.

One week later, I received a phone call from him asking whether I would be willing to meet with them. We met that week, and as we chatted I learned that he had become a Christian while serving two tours of duty in Afghanistan. She was raised Roman Catholic, including parochial school. They were looking for a place to worship and bring his two boys from a previous marriage. Then the conversation moved into our theology of marriage and sacraments. Neither felt comfortable taking the Lord's Supper, they said, but they would continue to worship.

Some months later, I learned they had already volunteered in our Wednesday night programming for children, and a few weeks after that I was pleased to see them come for Holy Communion for the first time. We met in anticipation of their joining, and I learned that he had never been baptized. He was taking the Lord's Supper without baptism! I wasn't sure what to do, but I knew our Lord would not want to exclude him. Just before receiving them into our congregation I had the pleasure of baptizing him.

* * *

"We have a problem, Pastor Mike," Shannon said. "Two of our new member/disciples[1] have never been baptized."

---

1. At St. Mark we adopted the use of member/disciple in our Constitution and By-Laws. This was a conscious decision by our leadership for two reasons. The first is that we wanted to affirm the faithfulness of our members who had led us to that point in our history. We wanted to show that the direction we were headed was not discontinuous from our past. The second reason we adopted this form of referral to our people was to make it clear that we would be a disciple-making ministry. Everything we did would be done with this goal in mind. Having come to the conclusion that the old "membership model" for ministry in the Protestant churches in the United States was no longer adequate for the challenges before us, we nonetheless wanted to acknowledge our history while pointing to our future. We recognize that this may seem cumbersome. On the other hand, we decided that it best expressed our gratitude for those who brought us to this place and time as well as point to the future we believed God was calling us to.

"We've already received them," I said. "I guess I'll have to call them and set a time for their baptisms."

"I'm sorry about that," Shannon continued. "When they turned in their data sheets they left the baptism information blank. I just assumed they didn't know. But when I called them, they told me they had never been involved in church before and hadn't been baptized."

"Well, we'll have to ask new questions, won't we?" I replied. "At least we're not just shuffling transfer papers with other congregations! But this means we have to set aside our usual assumptions."

"I guess so," she replied.

I called them and shared with them that in order to be a member of St. Mark Lutheran Church they would need to be baptized. I later met with first one and then the other with her fiancé. In that meeting, I learned that not only was she not baptized, but she wondered whether I would be willing to baptize her mother. I found out that her mother was attending a Christian church of another denomination but had never been baptized. When her daughter decided she was going to be baptized and asked her mother to attend church for it, her mother asked if she might be baptized at the same time.

Three weeks later, we had a wonderful experience of baptizing both mother and daughter in one of our regularly scheduled services. The following week, the other new member was baptized as well.

* * *

"Do we have non-member weddings here?" our new staff member asked. "Yes, we do," I replied. "But first we need to see if the date and time they want is available. Then they'll need to meet with either Pastor Dick or me to see if we will marry them. Then the wedding date, time, and pastor will be locked in."

"Oh. But his father is a Lutheran pastor and they'd like to have him perform the wedding." "In that case," I said, "get the information and I'll send a letter of invitation to him to perform the wedding at St. Mark. But they'll have to work with our wedding coordinator."

The letter was sent. The wedding was scheduled. Then, I received the call that the bride-to-be would like to be baptized and become a part of our congregation. A week later, after our last worship service had ended, the three of us stood at the font of God's love and she was baptized.

Old-World Habits

I often wonder what my bishop would say if he knew these things were going on. My ministry training prepared me for a much more traditional approach to membership. I was used to other Lutherans transferring into my church or practicing Christians from other denominations entering membership. Then, it was simply introducing them to Lutheran theology and the practices of a particular congregation. Until the past six years, I never worried about whether new members were baptized; I simply assumed they would be.

Nor was I prepared for the conversion to faith that we have experienced. People who have little or no biblical knowledge—with limited theological understanding—come to experience God and find the spiritual wherewithal to make it through the next week. Fractured families, couples cohabiting, personal crises—these are the stuff of the new world for which my old-world habits have simply not prepared me.

But I am not alone. In the past twenty years, according to official ELCA information, we have lost more than 50 percent of the attendance of children in our Sunday schools and vacation Bible schools. The average age of mainline Protestantism varies from sixty to sixty-five, and is aging. According to sociologist Robert Wuthnow, only about one in three of the young people we have confirmed are still in our denomination, and only 8 percent are attending any church at all! No wonder we are getting older.

Not only have we been unprepared for the twenty-first century, our churches cling to old-world habits like sailors clinging to any piece of timber after a shipwreck. I was recently startled when a layman from another Lutheran church, hearing that we have both traditional and contemporary worship at St. Mark, replied, "Well, we're going to do the Lutheran liturgy right until the last person in our church shuts the lights out." And they probably will.

At a conference I attended, Russell Crabtree of Holy Cow! Consulting challenged a group of pastors and spouses with the results of his significant study on congregations and satisfaction. This study found that the satisfaction level of a congregation is lower when the pastor is focused on pastoral care than when the pastor leads! The satisfaction level also increases with flexibility and decreases with social or theological rigidity.

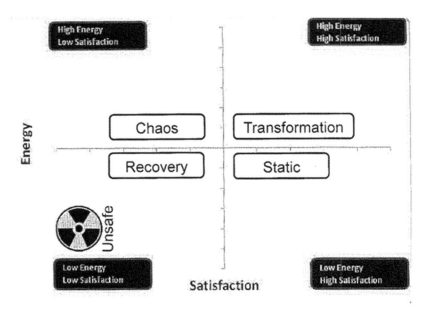

Figure 1

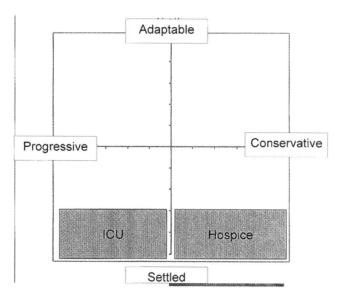

Figure 2

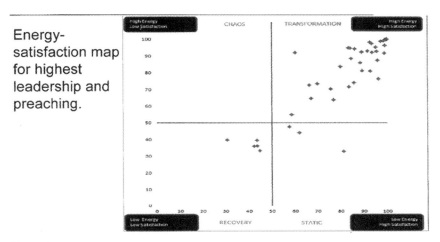

Energy-satisfaction map for highest leadership and preaching.

Figure 3

Our old-world habits were to focus on pastoral care as the major day-to-day function of a pastor. We were taught that theological clarity was critical for the well-being of our congregation. Neither Crabtree nor I are suggesting that pastoral care should be neglected or that theological clarity is unimportant. What his research suggests is that there is a collision between our old-world habits and effective ministry in this new age.

At St. Mark, our average age is thirty-six and we are growing younger. Our Sunday school has doubled in two years. Our average worship attendance has doubled as well. We are facing the challenge of limited resources (though giving has increased significantly!) and the need for adequate physical space. We have grown, with 60 percent of our new members coming from unchurched or dechurched situations. (The unchurched are those who have no formal or official Christian background; the dechurched are those who have attended a Christian church as children or adults but have not for ten years before coming to St. Mark.) The number of adult baptisms has been steady and strong, and we have had to move from three new member classes in a year to four. This is surely the work of the Holy Spirit!

We have not abandoned our theology. We have two traditional and two contemporary worship services each week, with one on Saturday night. We celebrate Holy Communion at each service every week. Our sermons last from eighteen to twenty minutes or more. We steadfastly keep our worship length to one hour, except on Wednesday night when we have an extended teaching service. We have a growing two-year confirmation ministry to which our young people habitually invite their friends.

What we are doing differently is opening up ministry to all of God's people. We are celebrating Luther's affirmation of the priesthood of believers. Both pastors make hospital calls, but the fabric of hospital care is woven by trained lay visitors and other members of our church. We encourage new ministry teams to come into being for the sake of a particular need and, when that need is met, to simply stop. We are committed to ongoing evaluation of our ministries. And yes, we "kill" ministries that are dead or dying.

We have found it necessary to be clear about our mission, vision, and values. These guide our decision making. We begin every staff meeting or church council meeting with a Bible study and read together our core values (Discipleship, Integrity, Community, Excellence), mission ("Grow in Faith, Share Jesus Christ, and Serve Others") and our vision ("Growing disciples across generations with real faith for real life"). And we welcome anyone that God sends to us, no matter where they are on their spiritual journey.

There are no cost-free decisions, and the decision to grow and reach out beyond the old-world habits that worked for a number of generations has not been without cost. We have lost members. As we have grown, the church has not remained the same. We have become more complex, and the expectations of our members have increased as we have become clear about our mission, vision, and values. The old ways of doing things no longer work. They didn't before, either, but the measuring stick then was not vitality but the comfort of those already present. Such a measuring stick only postpones the inevitable: growing smaller and older, with the dissatisfaction of knowing, unconsciously, that the congregation's days are numbered.

When we embarked upon our first building campaign, we lost a family. The reason was obvious: they didn't want to give any more. As we have worked hard to increase the value of our ministries—moving confirmation from a faith *information* system to a faith *transformation* system—we lost families. They nostalgically held the old catechism- and pastor-led preparation to be the litmus test of effective teen education. The fact that we retained few or none of our young people after confirmation had little bearing on their value for the "tried and true." When we moved to a more relationship-based confirmation, with the doctrinal information in the second year and the faith formation and biblical literacy in the first year, we began to build a bridge for our young people from confirmation into our senior high ministry. The goal was to make Christians, not just little Lutherans.

With the four-service schedule on weekends, there are those who complain that they don't know everyone anymore, that they don't see all their friends anymore. Yet our value of community has spawned a fellowship time between Sunday worship services that has exponentially increased the participation we now have. We have a single congregation with many expressions. But, frankly, any church that includes more than forty to fifty people already has more than one expression of their ministry; they just don't want to acknowledge it.

The breakthrough for ministry at St. Mark grew out of the partnership between the pastoral leadership and the congregation. The desire was for a church that could be a place where individuals and families would meet our God in worship, have opportunities to grow in faith and service, and develop Christian relationships. This desire compelled us to move beyond the historic activities or perspectives of the congregation. Lay leadership not only embraced but championed change. With congregations around us in serious decline or going out of business, the people of St. Mark made the conscious decision that they did not want that to be their future. We have worked hard to encourage everyone to move with us into the future. We have worked equally hard to make certain that our future was not held hostage to a particular individual or family with convictions or inclinations that went counter to who we believed God was calling us to be and become. Sadly but predictably, not everyone has chosen to be a part of this emerging future.

Leadership will be required in the twenty-first-century church to make these difficult choices. Clergy and laity will need to forge a partnership in mission based upon clearly identified and stated core values as well as a vision that leads into the future the Holy Spirit is calling the church to. Simply accepting the continuing decline and aging of our churches is neither biblical nor faithful. We are called to reinvent, with the Holy Spirit, the Protestant church in America. The only question is what is required of us and how we shall do it.

Two Necessary Convictions

The Christian church in the twenty-first century faces new opportunities and challenges. The confidence of congregational leaders for this new era of ministry will, I believe, be based upon two necessary convictions. The first is that, as the revealed truth of God, the gospel of Jesus Christ is the single most hope-filled, joy-producing, and faith-enriching message in the world. The second is that, apart from the basic faith tenets outlined in the Apostles' Creed, we no longer have all the questions, let alone answers, for effective ministry. For the sake of the timeless truth in Jesus Christ, we have to subject our methods and practices to critical evaluation and action. We must think of the congregation as a learning organization, able to test and respond to our changing context.

When we discovered that some of those we had already received as new members were not baptized, it challenged us at St. Mark to consider the possibility that our usual practice of receiving people was no longer adequate. Frankly, the question on our data form was assumed to be for information only. Historically, we assumed our new members had been baptized—usually as infants. So, leaving the baptismal information section blank was assumed to mean that they needed to talk to their parents to find out dates and locations. The experience I related above has been replicated at least twice since that original event. We have now learned that the questions we had asked were not sufficient to this new time of ministry. Since that time, we have had numerous adult baptisms—including one at a local lake because the young man of faith desired to be immersed. When he asked if that was something Lutherans did, I laughed and told him that the amount of water didn't matter. It was the water and the Word that mattered. Engagement with this young man and his faith led to articulating our understanding of the sacrament of holy baptism in a different language—but it was still the historic witness of our faith.

Such opportunities to serve and connect our faith to the lives of others will always be a collaborative process. This is true not just with those who are entering our congregations but also with leaders, members, and staff.

A young organist and choir director once asked me, "Do you really ask your choirmaster and organist to pick the hymns for your worship?" The question emerged out of a workshop hosted at St. Mark for organists and choir directors in the central United States, with participants from Iowa, Kansas, and Nebraska.

"Yes," I replied. "I learned a few years ago that I want to involve our musicians in the planning of worship as early as possible. I want their input in the shaping of things—whether that is our contemporary or traditional worship leader."

"But what if they have a different point of view or disagree with the direction you're taking?" she continued. "Wouldn't you just make a decision and put an end to it?"

"Well, I want to have the conversation. We are clear about authority and responsibility, so I know that they understand the decision is finally mine. But I want them to have ownership of the direction, too. Being a pastor is hard enough without having to be perfect and make all the decisions. After all," I continued, "what if they're right and I am wrong?"

There was silence. Then one of the organists said, "Most of us here have never heard our pastor suggest that they might be wrong."

For collaboration in ministry to succeed, the parties involved have to admit that they need one another, that no one has all the answers, that all are learning together. Christian partnership has the added benefit of acknowledging that each is gifted, and those gifts ought to be available for the sake of the ministry of the church. This is Luther's understanding of the priesthood of all believers.

I am convinced that the pastoral perspective on worship will be enhanced by the gifts and understanding of capable musicians. In my own ministry there have been countless times when, without having seen the hymn or praise song beforehand, I have been lifted up in worship by the music chosen by our music leaders. The melodies or lyrics fit so powerfully with the theme of the day that I lose myself in worship and, for just a moment, forget that I am leading. More importantly, I am grateful that I do not work alone but with others committed to giving their best for the sake of worshiping our God. In those moments, I know I couldn't have done as good a job as they did.

For the sake of God's truth in Jesus Christ we must begin to think of the church as a learning organization. We are in a time like no other. We cannot possibly know what the issues will be, let alone the answers to them. When we think of the church as a learning organization we begin to open ourselves to God's future. We don't expect perfection of ourselves (a denial of grace!), but strive to grow through our mistakes and successes. The church as a learning organization embraces grace: we are not perfect and we will not pretend to be. When this happens, we no longer need to defend our tradition or methods. We are open to asking about the goal, and how we can best achieve it in Jesus' name.

This grace-filled attitude begins as the soul work of the pastor who is the chief leader in the church.

2

The Pastor's Soul: Leaning on Grace

Faith that is put into practice is a living faith. The life of discipleship begins in the mind and heart of the leader, and then becomes the foundation upon which ministry is built. In this chapter, I will identify and demonstrate the practices of discipleship. This is not a complete explication of the many ways they can be practiced. Rather, I invite the reader into the inner journey of the soul. This is the invitation of God's grace in Jesus Christ. This is also the "inside-out" leadership that will stand the test of time.

I hope the reader will see this chapter as an invitation to the circle of faith formation instead of a list to be checked off. In my experience, there are times when one practice is stronger than another; one expression of faith more easily accessed than another. The invitation is to spiritual growth and depth. Facing the present challenges requires an inner strength and focus that is best nurtured in private practice and within the community of the local congregation.

Imperfect Faith

The wonderful thing about faith is that it is imperfect.

A father brought his son to be healed of a demon that would seize the boy and throw him into a fit. At times the boy would be thrown into the fire. Jesus, up on the Mount of Transfiguration, came down to find his disciples arguing since no one could free the child. The boy's father approached Jesus and explained the situation, saying that the demon had tormented the boy since childhood. "It has often cast him into the fire and into the water, to destroy him; but if you are able to do anything, have pity on us and help us." Jesus said to him, "If you are able!—All things can be done for the one who believes." The father cried out, "I believe; help my unbelief." And Mark records that Jesus cast the demon out and healed the child (Mark 9:14-29).

There are few events in the life of Jesus of Nazareth that express the dynamic of faith like this one. The father, desperate to save his boy, has brought him to Jesus' disciples in the hope—the faith!—that his child could be made well. The disciples were in over their heads. Jesus challenges the father to trust in God. The father, at his wit's end, expresses the cry of so many of us: "How much more faith must I have? Help me, O Lord, to have that much faith."

Pastors are no longer called to be the public ideal of faith. Instead, the twenty-first-century church leader is called to stand authentically beside the people of God as they struggle with faith. The distance between the ideal and the real is no longer acceptable—if it ever was! People of the church need to know that their pastor believes in God as revealed in Jesus Christ. They also need to know that he or she understands the imperfection of faith. The truth is that we do not believe as we should. We all believe as we are able. And the gospel is that God, in Jesus Christ, meets us there—just as the Savior met that father so long ago. This fundamental grace of God is the source of the pastor's continued service—whether preaching or teaching; serving communion or saying the prayers of commendation for the dying; baptizing a child in the bloom of new life or officiating at the memorial service. Pastors, like that father, lean on grace: the accepting, loving presence of the Savior Jesus.

Personal Practices of Faith

When pastors accept that imperfection is the nature of faith, then we can begin to grow in our confidence with God and before the people of God. Our ministry is no longer based solely upon our abilities but is founded on the God who works through imperfect people to accomplish the perfect work of faith. Faith is God's work, not ours. At best, we can point toward it. That is our task, to point and say, "See here . . . or there? That is the living power of God's love for imperfect people. And I am first among them."

We cannot give what we do not have. None of us has a perfect faith. Faith begins with our imperfection, and then the Holy Spirit meets us in the perfect love of God. We, at best, give imperfect witness to God's perfect will—even when we do not understand it. Then we call others to seek and find this God-man Jesus. The pastor's practices of faith both ground and strengthen this calling. We dare to trust that in our imperfect words and deeds the perfect love of God can become present to others through the work of the Holy Spirit.

Years ago, I formed an acrostic to guide my personal practices of faith and to equip others for their journey into discipleship: POWER SURGE. The vowels drop off, leaving the first letters of the practices described below: PWRSRG. Over the past few years, this acrostic has proven helpful to many congregations, pastors, and lay leaders. For a more in-depth treatment, see my book *Power Surge: Six Marks of Discipleship for a Changing Church.*

Pray Daily

Prayer is the beginning of our task. These are not the prayers we pray in our official capacity. Instead, these are our own private and personal prayers. Sometimes they take the form of the historic church and are formal. In these instances, it is as if the believers of long past express the longings of our souls. In the twists and turns of ministry, I have found historic prayer to have a depth of meaning unmatched by my paltry pleadings with God.

> O God, you have called your servants to ventures of which we cannot see the ending, by paths as yet untrodden, through perils unknown. Give us faith to go out with good courage, not knowing where we go, but only that your hand is leading us and your love supporting us; through Jesus Christ our Lord. Amen. (ELW, pg. 304)

When I pray this prayer, I am reminded that I cannot control tomorrow. I do not know what challenges and joys will meet me because I will follow paths unknown to me. But I can trust the God of my journey. There are prayers in our traditional worship services that seem dry as dust, relics of our liturgical past. But there are other formal prayers that seem to embody the faith and point to our Lord Jesus in ways that defy language. These are the prayers of worship that are the heart-felt prayers of the worship leader.

Then there are the deeply personal prayers of the pastor that will never be heard by anyone other than our God. These embody our struggles of faith; they give expression to the groans of our hearts in the face of tragedy; they storm the gates of heaven on behalf of a critical need in the life of the pastor or another. They can be as silent as the dusk or as loud as a widow's wail. Like the prayer of the father in Mark's Gospel, they are always at the intersection of a faith that dares to believe and circumstances that assert the absence of God—not just our God, but any god at all.

* * *

When Jennifer could not stand in worship for the opening hymn, she quietly sat down. As our worship continued, she became aware of her growing weakness and dizziness. Then, when communion was being served, she realized she could not go forward. That's when her daughter called 911. As the final hymn was being sung, the EMTs arrived. During the final verse, they put Jennifer on the gurney and exited the worship space.

Over the next few days, one of our lay ministers remained with Jennifer and her family members. I, as pastor on call, visited with her in support. Then, as I arrived at about 3:30 one afternoon, a closed door to Jennifer's hospital room stopped me. Two hospital technicians explained that the doctor was in the room, had been for quite awhile, and would surely soon be out. When her physician came out of her room, he closed the door. "I'm her pastor," I said. "Can I go in?" "Please do," he responded, and opened the door.

I entered a scene of shock. She had just heard that what had appeared to be a simple problem with blood pressure was in fact a cancerous tumor putting pressure on her aortal artery and kidneys. After a lengthy time of listening and caring, I prayed and left.

All the way back to the church, I kept picturing Jennifer kindly serving at church, watering the plants, stuffing the bulletins, hosting events. How could this happen to such a wonderful person? I asked. And I pictured the Savior gently telling the woman with a twelve-year hemorrhage that she would be well. In the face of daunting news, with no prognosis available, I dared to claim such a healing for her. Then, realizing that prayer is not control over God but access to God's love, I simply entrusted her into his care. "I believe; help my unbelief."

These ongoing conversations with God often constitute the lifeblood of faith for the pastoral leader. The nearness of our holy God brings with it the trust that this God is the one who loves us and, like a loving parent, wants to hear our heartfelt desires—not just what we think we ought to pray for. And if we can have such an active relationship with God, then we know that others can as well. We speak of what we know: the Lord Jesus Christ meets us where we are, not where we ought to be. Real faith is imperfect.

The various prayers of the pastor will, sooner or later, become the deeds of faith. To pray is to eventually do. An example of this came one year when we celebrated Christmas in October. Our congregation had been walking through the compact Bible entitled *The Story*, and we transitioned from the Old Testament to the birth of the Messiah in the fall. As we reflected on the Savior's birth, I challenged us all to not only receive the gift of the Babe of Bethlehem but to become the gift of God's love in the world through surprising acts of kindness.

Soon after, I turned into the drive-through at my favorite Starbucks, inadvertently cutting off another vehicle I hadn't seen coming. As I ordered, I thought of the sermon—as well as the woman's surprised and unhappy face as I cut her off—and prayed that I might surprise her with grace, if not a concrete apology. So I paid the barista for her order.

Prayer can sometimes take concrete form—like buying coffee for a stranger. I wanted to "be the gift" and, at the same time, apologize. I do not know whether these goals were accomplished, but whether my prayer would be turned into action was within my power to determine.

As another example, sometimes when I am out for a jog, I'll think of someone I know who cannot run—and I turn my run into a prayer. "Lord Jesus," I will pray, "let every step I take be a prayer for somebody that they may be blessed and know the healing power of your love." Sound silly? No more so than the habit of using prayer beads for praying. And the benefit to me is the awareness of the presence of God and the desire to extend it to someone else.

Worship Weekly

Actions become prayers when we consciously offer them to God—which is, of course, the basis for Christian worship. "Liturgy" comes from two Greek words: *laos*, meaning people, and *ergon*, meaning work. So liturgy is "the work of the people." Yet for most of us as pastors (as well as some of our key lay leaders), it is our work. We take responsibility to see that the preparations are done well, that the participants all know their role and are capable of them, that the music will work with the theme of the message or liturgical day, and that we have done our work. Then we shepherd the service. The problem is that our work frequently excludes the possibility that we might actually worship!

Christian leadership is doing the right thing at the right time. This is no truer than in worship. That means there are times when we will have to exercise a hands-on approach to leading worship. We are all too familiar with the soloist who didn't sufficiently rehearse or the children's program that disintegrates in front of us. The pastor will need to intervene—if possible!—or, at the least, learn from such experiences how to better ensure that they will not happen again. And there have been times when pastors will need to interrupt for the sake of the worshipers.

I'll never forget watching a volunteer consistently undermine the flow of our worship by changing our worship slides late. At St. Mark we have a lovely sanctuary in which a large screen is placed above and behind the altar. This allows our worshipers to see the words of our prayers as well as our contemporary hymns. But this Sunday, our volunteer would wait for the last word of any given slide to be said before changing to the next one. This meant a delay as we continued—again and again.

Between the services, I went upstairs to our media center and asked the volunteer to *please* move to the next slide while we said the second to the last word on the slide before us. It worked—until Monday morning, when I received a very angry phone call telling me that I had ruined the experience of that volunteer. In retrospect, perhaps I could have used gentler language—frankly, I couldn't remember exactly what I had said. On the other hand, the experience of the worship for the next two services improved significantly.

Doing the right thing at the right time may require intervention. On the other hand, sometimes it means letting go and worshiping. I have come to believe that the first and best thing worship leaders can do is to enter into worship themselves. What we do is so often what we can give. When we are able to worship, we can authentically invite others into worship. Whenever possible, I will pray before our worship services: "Lord Jesus, help us do the very best we can so that we can get out of your way to do what only you can do." Worship may be the work of the people, but it is only possible by the presence and touch of the Holy Spirit. The discipline of worship leadership also includes the inner focus of worship for the leader.

There are those moments when I am lifted out of my concerns and vigilance in worship. As mentioned earlier, I do not choose the hymns or contemporary songs of praise for our worship. Instead, I trust our worship leaders to make those decisions. We all are committed to working together so that the single focal point of our worship services is upheld in word and song. As a result, I often find myself surprised by what has been selected. Whether it is a traditional hymn or a contemporary song of praise, my surprise will delight me, drive me inward and I will lose myself in worship. When that happens, everything changes about the service for me. Now I know it has moved from being our work to becoming the work of the Holy Spirit.

I believe worship leaders long for such moments. I have never met a pastor who became a pastor without experiencing them. Yet I have heard many pastors lament that they cannot worship on Sunday with the people they are serving. This is both tragic and unnecessary. Let the pastor do her work, equip those who are serving in worship to do theirs, and then relax and trust the working of the Holy Spirit. Let worship surprise us with God's grace! Look and plan for those moments of delight or the humbling of the soul. Leading worship means worshiping—not just working.

This is why I attend church while I'm on vacation. I believe that God has created humankind for worship; that is, with a space deeply within each of us that can only be touched and satisfied by our worshiping. And when I worship, I try to come with an open mind and spirit. Most of the time, I am able to hear the word spoken, prayed, and sung in such a way that my soul is fed. When I can't keep an open mind and spirit, on that rare occasion that the pastor struggles with his message, I pray for the minister and the congregation. And I look for those elements in the service that can touch me with God's grace.

A number of years ago, I attended a service where the pastor was doing a fine job of preaching. The topic and presentation were interesting and engaging. Then she said something that I just couldn't agree with. I found myself arguing with her in my mind. After worship, my wife asked what I thought of the sermon and, after complimenting the pastor on her topic and presentation, I shared with my wife that I just couldn't agree with a statement she had made. My wife laughed and said she knew that would get me. Then she told me some of the other things that pastor had gone on to say that my wife found to be delightful—a real blessing. That's when I realized I hadn't heard anything after that one sentence—I had become derailed and hadn't heard much of anything after that.

I was embarrassed, and I felt cheated. That's when I decided I'd try to set aside those things that I disagreed with in a colleague's sermon in order to hear her out. I keep working at it so that I can worship—which, of course, is the point.

Read the Bible Daily

When I announced at St. Mark that I wanted to put Bibles in the racks of our pews and chairs so that anyone who wanted a new Bible could take one, I was pleasantly surprised by the response. When I said that we didn't have the money in the budget so I was looking for generous gifts to cover the cost, I was even more surprised by the generous response. We have used these Bibles in our worship and have given so many away that we have had to replenish the Bibles in our sanctuary four or five times already.

We are deliberate in how we use God's word. Because we live in a biblically ignorant age, at St. Mark we only use one Scripture passage for each service. On occasion this changes, but that is our standard practice. We know that multiple texts and a psalm are the norm, but have chosen to focus on one passage of Scripture so that everyone knows what we are talking about. I will invite those in worship to take out the sanctuary Bibles (or their own) and turn to the passage for the day. And, since most adults are not used to working with the Bible, we publish the text and the page numbers in the sanctuary Bibles where they can easily find it. Our hope is that if people really need comfort or strengthening in their personal life, they'll feel comfortable looking in God's word.

That's where I often go. I have found that my ministry loses its focus and bearings when I am not personally reading and reflecting on God's word. Gerhard Ebeling, in his masterful book *Toward a Theological Theory of Language*, shared a model for Luther's interpreting Scripture. This model holds the written word accountable to the Living Word, Jesus. This model shapes my own personal and professional use of the Scriptures. I try to read the written passage of Scripture in its historical context, but when I need spiritual encouragement or sustenance, I read to meet the God of Jesus Christ in the Bible.

My personal use of the Bible is the foundation for my professional use. I look to meet Jesus in the Bible. I pray that others will meet Christ in the Scriptures as I teach or proclaim them, with the primary goal of helping others experience the presence of Christ in their lives. This is not to be confused with being overly emotional. Instead, I believe it is facilitated by striving to hold in tension critical thinking and inspiration. My study in preparation for sermons or Bible studies tilts to the academic. I try to work in the original languages when I can. I have a library of secondary sources from a variety of perspectives for additional insight and commentary. During the coffee time between services, a man approached me and said, "Pastor Mike, I want you to know that I can't daydream anymore during sermons. When you preach, I have to pay attention and think."

"Thank you," I responded. "I take that as a compliment." To which he replied, "I'm not sure I intended it as a compliment."

I cannot read the Bible without reflecting on myself and life as I know it and live it. I heard that man suggesting that such reflection isn't always easy, and it shouldn't be. Most of us grow intellectually and spiritually when we are uncomfortable. This discomfort opens us to changing perspectives and behaviors. The paradox is that such discomfort will lead us to the comfort of the gospel. Both require the same conviction: in the Bible we are being addressed by the living God revealed in Jesus Christ and active through the Holy Spirit. If the Bible has little or no authority, then we will experience neither the holy discomfort of reflecting on our lives nor the comfort of God's love and acceptance when we need it the most.

Leading through God's word recognizes and articulates this claim of authority—not just for worshipers but for the leader. Without such a claim of authority, there is no point to preaching or teaching the Bible except as vapid literature or a book of interesting stories and insights. I am not suggesting that every pastor or leader in Christ's church agrees with my understanding of the authority of Scripture, but the leader will need to clearly understand and articulate her own convictions about the authority of the Bible and how that encourages spiritual growth.

Neither am I suggesting that there is a "once and for all time" understanding of this authority. Our appreciation of the authority of the Bible often changes over time. Reflecting on God's word and its claim of authority will be challenged in difficult circumstances and strengthened in times of needed assurance. A pastor's sense of the authority of the Bible will be applied in different ways in different circumstances. For example, while I would not argue with the theory of evolution as the method God chose for God's ongoing creation, I would argue that an intelligent will, who I know as God, is in fact our Creator. I would not look to the Bible as a substitute for psychiatric counsel and care. I would assert that the Bible can help engender healthy attitudes and behaviors that can bring a healthy balance to life, and comfort and belonging to those who struggle with mental illness. The authority of the Bible, I am suggesting, underlies the pastor's personal and professional use of it. It can be nuanced for particular circumstances, but the underlying assumption of authority still needs to be addressed by the pastor in order to effectively use God's word—personally or professionally.

Serve within and beyond the Congregation

They shuffled into the Salvation Army dining room for a Thanksgiving meal complete with turkey and stuffing, mashed potatoes and gravy, sweet potatoes and string beans and pumpkin pie with whipped cream. These homeless folks were in a rush—many having stood waiting for over an hour. My job was to welcome them with a smile and a handshake. I stood and grinned and welcomed people who took my hand, said, "Thank you," and, no matter how hard I tried, never looked me in the eye.

Then a family of four came in: Mom and Dad pushing a little boy and girl forward. So I knelt down and, catching the little boy's eye, smiled and said, "Happy Thanksgiving. We're so glad you're here." That little boy, still unmarred by the experience of living in his car, smiled, took my hand and said, "Thank you." I stayed on my knee and, looking up, caught the father's eye. He smiled and repeated my greeting. For the first time that morning, an adult looked me in the eye and responded. From that time on, I always dipped down to catch the eyes of those who habitually looked down in shame. In this way, I could greet these nameless, faceless lost ones by looking up at them, not looking down on them. Later, I thought that for many of them this might have been the first position of power they had experienced in a very long time. And my heart was glad.

Jesus commands his followers to lead by serving. Since that experience at the Salvation Army, I have concluded that service grows the soul strong. It takes a strong heart to serve from a humble position. It takes a willing heart to take what needs doing and make it your own. That's the invitation to pastors who follow Jesus: "Come and grow a strong heart from a willing heart," he seems to say, "and you'll never be the same, never see the same, again."

Christian leaders serve both within and beyond the congregation. The first is the opportunity close at hand. The second is the challenge of stretching out of the ordinary, but that is where you'll meet the extraordinary. I don't know if anyone of those who met me that Thanksgiving morning met Christ in me. I do know that I met Christ on the growing, serving edge.

When I came to St. Mark, it took me a number of weeks to discover that over the doorway leading to the parking lot hangs a sign that says, "Now let the service begin." I have no idea how many times I walked underneath that sign and never saw it. When I did see it, it told me of the serving heart of the people of our congregation. That serving heart is demonstrated weekly, whether it is serving a meal at the homeless shelter downtown, collecting underwear or outer garments for those who are in desperate need, or collecting school supplies for children in our community who otherwise would go without. Serving is not what a Christian leader does—it is who he is. And the congregation that embodies such faith is an invitation and attraction to those who visit or learn about them.

The Christian congregation that doesn't serve will soon not like itself. This dislike will metastasize into a chronic distrust of themselves and the leader, often leading to internal conflicts that are both unnecessary and unsolvable because the issues involved in the conflicts are not the real problem. Christians know that service is necessary to our faith. The pastor who leads with service is putting into place a habit of health for the church. Stories of service that reflect to the congregation its own involvement and the blessed outcomes from it nurture an appropriate self-confidence in the church that will multiply itself over time.

Christ's command to serve is an affirmation that people have been created to serve. The data is clear: the healthiest and most joy-filled people are those who habitually serve. They are engaged in their community, interact with people through shared purpose, and can see and feel the impact of their serving in the lives of others—beginning with themselves. This is how God intended it to be. Leadership in the twenty-first-century church stands and works beside those who serve.

As congregations expand their involvement in serving the community, they will begin to hear the call to go and serve beyond their nation. They will develop a strategy for global engagement that fits their mission and vision. Leaders will first visit the site, get to know their partners, and then return with others to serve. One of the axioms of twenty-first-century Christian leadership is that our money follows our people. As the people are engaged in serving, the church can stand alongside them through special offerings or by adding a budgeted line item. Either way, the principle is demonstrated.

The function of leadership in these areas is often to catch up to others and bless their work. Our people will often hear of a need and have their hearts touched before the pastor will. The temptation for leaders is to see first why it can't happen, instead of working to see how it might happen in an effective and meaningful way. The strains on church budgets are very real and an additional demand for support—even just the involvement of people—can seem threatening to one who is trying to keep everyone together and going in the same direction.

Leaders can expect that any service requires three key elements in order to be fully endorsed by the congregation. First, a team must be created to address the need. Second, financial support will initially have to come from outside the budget. Third, the team will need to show how this particular service opportunity fits within the values, vision, and mission of the church. If any of these elements cannot be organized or articulated, then—though the service opportunity may be a very good thing—the time is not right for the congregation to endorse it. I have watched as missions unfolded over time after two or three efforts to create a team, find the initial funding, and align it with the focal points of the congregation.

Leaders know that good is no substitute for best. This is true in many aspects of our ministries, but it is critical for serving. The reason for this is the incredible amount of good causes that strive for our attention and support every day. For the church's mission to stand out, it must be clear, focused, and have the support of an engaged team, not just an individual.

Relate to Others for Spiritual Growth

The demands of leadership bring a host of temptations. One of these is the temptation to do good things without conversation and support from our key relationships, beginning with our own family.

The Pastor's Family

The story of two people I know began at church; she was involved in the ministry to women and he in worship and teaching. As the senior pastor, he was busy on Sundays and, often, with meetings during the week. He led semi-annual mission trips to Central America and she stayed home. Over the years, their relationship slipped into a comfortable rhythm. On the surface, things seemed perfect. It came as a shock when he was publicly exposed as having an affair with one of the office staff.

He said it started with a deep loneliness that he couldn't understand or articulate. He never tried to explain it to his wife. Instead, he said, they fought over trivialities as a way of fending one another off. By the time the affair began, he and his wife were roommates instead of spouses. The intimacy and close friendship they had known was lost in the busy schedules and public images they maintained.

He lost his ministry. He lost his wife and children. After two years, he lost the secretary he had married in the aftermath. He's rebuilding his life working in sales.

Twenty-first-century Christian leaders understand that leadership can be lonely. Difficult and painful decisions will need to be made, and leaders need confidants and life partners with whom these can be shared. The spouse will need to learn not to try and solve things or provide easy answers. The ministry brings us into relationships with many people, and our unattended needs can create a vulnerability of which we may be unaware. We will be invited into situations that will stretch our healthy boundaries. Add to this the fact that we live in a sexually insistent age, and the elements are in place for the tragedy of what my friend lived through.

Two key relationships need to be clearly identified and our commitments made clear. The first, of course, is our relationship with God—which is not to be confused with our relationship to the church. I have already discussed some of the elements of a healthy ongoing relationship with our God.

The second is with our spouse and family—assuming we have not been called to the ministry of the celibate. Early on, pastors need to separate their commitments to their families from their calling to ministry. At the seminary I attended, we were privileged to have the wisdom of Dr. Lee Griffin, psychiatrist and man of faith. He challenged us to remember that our calling to our spouses trumped the calling to ministry. This was essential, he asserted, because without that clarity our work in the church could become a substitute for our spouse. This was confirmed after I had been serving in my first call when a wise pastor confided to me that "ministry is a jealous mistress who will take as much time and energy as you are willing to give." Learning to say yes to his wife, he said, meant learning when to say no to the church.

Things haven't changed in this regard. Pastors, you must make the decision to honor your relationship with your spouse by working through the difficult issues of ministry and family on a regular basis. Make the commitment to nurture your relationship with planned times away for the intimacy that is so essential to healthy relationships. This will provide a significant safeguard to your ministry. If you come to the tragic realization that the marriage isn't working, you must work on that separately from your ministry.

When my children were in grade school, my wife took a job as a teacher in a community about twenty-five miles from the town in which we lived. That meant that I was primary parent during the day. Once, I remember receiving a call that one of my daughters was sick with the flu. It came while I was in an executive committee meeting at our church. I explained the circumstances to the lay leaders around me and they graciously told me to go take care of my child. Our meeting was rescheduled for another day. During those formative years, There were times when investing in the lives of my children was easy. There were times when it was intrusive. That's what children are: easy and intrusive.

My wife and I decided to try to live a "normal life" even though I was in ministry. We tried to keep our family separate so that our children would not grow up labeled as "preacher's kids." We didn't want our children so enmeshed in the ministry that they experienced inappropriate expectations from the members of our congregation. I suspect they were aware of these expectations anyway. Nevertheless, by working in that direction we made a commitment to our children that we hoped would provide a "normal" life for them. Pastors need to be aware of these dynamics and decide to preserve their family from the sometimes-excessive demands of the parish.

The Pastor and Small Groups

Caring for the people of God can create pseudo-relationships. It can provide the illusion of friendship where acquaintanceship actually exists. To counter that natural misunderstanding, I have sought to be involved in small groups as well as identify three to five male prayer partners with whom I can establish a relationship of trust and confidentiality.

The idea of small groups, not as an add-on to ministry but as a vital part of the warp and weft of the church, is based upon Jesus' work with the Twelve. Small groups become the incubator of faith and promote spiritual and relationship growth. Small groups at St. Mark gather around topics that are often congregation-wide in scope. This doesn't mean that groups cannot choose their own material; they are free to do so. Rather, by inviting all of our small groups to gather around a congregation-wide study, we create a shared experience for all. The outcome of this has been a strengthening of the ministry as well as the leader's ability to shape the conversation about faith for the whole church.

Out of these small groups, systems of care also emerge. As congregations grow, it is increasingly impossible for the pastor to provide quality care to all. Small groups provide personal knowledge about individuals to those who then can provide personal care. This doesn't mean the pastor will not provide care. It means that the pastor is involved where the need demands the pastor's skill and care. My experience with small groups is that they will instinctively call on the pastor when needed. Otherwise, they simply reach out in Christian love to one another, and the support we all need is close at hand.

The pastor's involvement in a small group is critical for two reasons. First, the pastor will need to model the church she is seeking to help create. The pastor's involvement in small groups is critical if they are to become a building block for the church's ministry. The integrity of the pastor's vision is strengthened when she participates in ministry as she asks others to.

Second, pastors need the support and care of others just like anyone else. The number-one problem among clergy, in my observation, is loneliness. This can be addressed through committed participation in a small group. But this requires the pastor's commitment to finding a small group where the participants can accept her as a person—not just the pastor. This is problematic in that there are some members of our churches who will never be able to see beyond the role of pastor to care for the person. If that is the case in a small group, the pastor will need to start or find a new group. The rationale for this move can be framed so that it is not a rejection of the small group she is leaving. Instead, it embodies the principle that we all need to help create more small groups. Although there may be misunderstandings around this decision, the pastor simply needs to reiterate the vision and the rationale in the face of such misunderstanding and not get caught up in it. The reason is the health and well-being of the pastor and her spouse.

There are three criteria that I use in forming a small group for myself. First, I look for people whose work life or professional study equips them to understand confidentiality. The pastor will need to share things that have to stay in the small group in order for him to become a true participant. Those who, by training or experience, deal consistently with confidentiality will be most likely to allow the pastor this necessary privilege. Obviously, the pastor will need to exercise discretion in the sharing of such experiences, omitting names and details that could compromise another person's position in the church or his relationship with others. But this can be done.

Second, the people must have a perspective of the church beyond the particular congregation the pastor is serving. In other words, they need to bring experience from other congregations or ministries into the small group. This allows the pastor to share without everything being applied to that congregation alone. There have been some, in my experience, whose experience has been that congregation alone and who can allow the pastor to be real and honestly share—but very few. Without a larger perspective and experience of the church, the pastor's sharing can so easily be judged on whether it is complimentary to the congregation—even when that isn't a part of his sharing.

Lastly, I have found the criterion of similar age and family setting to be very helpful. When my wife and I were younger and had our children at home, we needed others who dealt with the issues we struggled with in our small group. Now that we are "empty nesters," we find that those pre-retirement empty nesters in our congregation can hear our concerns, joys, and hopes with greater understanding than others.

These criteria can be articulated in the vision of small groups. They are not "laws," but form a helpful checklist in the formation of groups. Obviously, participation in the life and ministry of the church is a starting point, unless the small group has decided ahead of time to be an outreach or evangelistic group.

These criteria are part of my selection of prayer partners as well. To them I add the requirement that they be of the same gender I am. Spirituality, sensuality, and sexuality are closely linked. I find men who have demonstrated wisdom, a personal prayer and faith life, and whose confidentiality is unquestionable. Presently, my three prayer partners include a physician, a therapist who manages a clinic, and a retired executive who managed significant projects and a large number of people. These three can be trusted to hear me out, value my opinion, and join me in prayer. I consider that, apart from my marriage and the accountability to the church council, these are those to whom I am personally accountable. They have helped me see things differently. They have strengthened my resolve in making hard decisions and supported me in my personal struggles. I cannot imagine a pastor being healthy without individuals like these in their lives. The process and criteria are critical, and the relationships will grow as they are tested over time.

A Vision for Small Groups

The question this conversation usually elicits is, "What is your vision for small group ministry in the congregation?" I believe that we live in a high-tech, low-touch world. Many in our time are confusing social media contact with person-to-person relationships, but they are not the same. One of the key differences is anonymity. With person-to-person relationships, like those formed in small groups, anonymity gives way to being truly known. In small groups, we have the opportunity to experience the acceptance and care of the church as we become transparent. This means, of course, that healthy small groups work within the context of a shared confidentiality. When we can trust that our hopes and needs can be shared with those who care about us and that they will stay in the group, we can let others into our lives at a deeper level. This safe space within the local congregation is a treasure for most pastors and congregational leaders. We are used to putting on a necessary, public face. That needs to stay in place as we fulfill the duties and obligations of our roles, but we need someplace where we can be real. A healthy small group allows that—and it can be grown within the church.

Healthy small groups have three components: heart, hands, and head. By *heart* I mean intentionally creating the atmosphere where people can share with one another, pray for one another, and check in on one another without feeling intrusive. The result is the growth of a community of care as part of the local congregation.

After I had shared with my small group that I was struggling with some management issues, a member of the group approached me and asked how I was doing. He knew that these issues included a difficult staff conflict that I was going to address the week following our small group meeting. He also knew that the details of it couldn't be shared; it was a personnel issue and therefore confidential. His concern was genuine; he didn't ask what I did or even if the situation had been resolved. He had learned that in our small group the care we give is about the person, not a particular situation.

"Thanks for asking," I replied. "I'm actually doing well. The situation was dealt with and the conversation, though heated at times, turned out to be a good thing for both of us."

"Well, I just wanted you to know that I was praying for you," he said.

I have met pastors who have never had that level of trust in a member of their church. I have also met pastors for whom no one in their church has ever prayed. How tragic! I believe we *are* the church with one another and for one another. Effective small groups nurture safe and healthy ways for that reality to be experienced.

The *hands* element comes when the members of the small group serve together. This can be within the congregation or outside the church. Every year we have a Saturday for the "hanging of the greens"—decorating the church for the Advent-Christmas season. When the volunteer recruited to lead that event went back to work and couldn't organize or participate, I asked small groups to take responsibility for decorating particular areas of our buildings. What a great job they did! Serving with one another in our small groups deepens relationships and connects the group to the Lord's command to serve. Something happens when the members of a small group band together in Christian service. The pastor steps alongside the other members of his small group in serving meals at the local homeless shelter and the bonds between the members who have served deepen. When the pastor has the opportunity to share this experience with the rest of the church, serving is no longer something the pastor preaches about. Now it is part of his faith, part of the small group ministry, and an expectation for all.

The *head* element is the biblical and theological component. Sometimes this can be a shared book. At other times it may be reflecting upon a biblical study that engages the group. This provides a focus for the meeting and, especially for most men, moves the small group past the "touchy feely" stuff so that everyone can contribute to the conversation.

The problem most pastors have in small groups that focus on biblical/theological content is that we are perceived as the resident expert. This dampens conversation and limits sharing. If the pastor takes care to help set up the conversation so that it is a sharing of ideas and perceptions, not a right or wrong discovery, that is often enough to open the group up. There will be times, however, when the pastor's knowledge and training will especially equip her to add to the discussion. This can be very helpful.

Effective small group ministry is the incubator of faith. Many adults in our congregations have never had the opportunity to think beyond their Sunday school theology within a church setting. It can be incredibly liberating when that happens. And when a pastor "models" that small groups are important and that questions are to be respected in them, the member/disciples within the church are invited to grow. The pastor's involvement in a small group authenticates the value of small groups for all.

* * *

I once heard an inspirational speaker say, "Christians should have long faces—not north and south, but east and west!" I can't remember the source, but I have not forgotten the words. Play is an important part of small groups. Being able to go to a ballgame or bowling or have a night out with one another helps build real relationships. When people in the congregation see a pastor enjoying herself or competing like everyone else, their perception of the pastor changes. This may be threatening to some who feel the need to maintain their distance from the members of their church, but I have found that it doesn't diminish the regard for my ministry at all. In fact, I have often said that the only thing I ever got from the pastor's pedestal was a nosebleed!

The pastor's faith is an expressed reality. For many in the congregation, our faith gains authenticity when they see us as regular people. That encourages them in turn to dare express their faith. There are risks to this humanizing of the pastor's faith, but the greater risk is an incipient loneliness than can erode the heart and soul of the leader. Implementing an effective small group ministry reduces the risk and increases the health component of our ministry.

Give a Tithe or Beyond

"You don't tithe, do you Pastor Mike?" He was the church treasurer, and he knew what my salary was as well as what we gave. It was a rhetorical question.

"No," I replied. "I don't believe in it."

"If I could show you that it is biblical, would you do it?" he asked. Just out of seminary, I was arrogant enough to believe that I knew better than he did—until he presented me with two pages of Bible passages that referenced tithing as an expectation of faith. At the time, my wife and I were giving about 3 percent to the church. Over the next five years, we moved to giving 10 percent of our take-home pay to the congregation. We still do. In fact, the tithe is the foundation of our giving, not the ceiling. My wife and I tithe to the local congregation, but we also give, as we are able, to a number of other charities as well as family members in need. This is not a basis for spiritual pride. Instead, I see it as a basic practice of my faith. My wife agrees. For us, it is a matter of integrity.

The ministry of the Christian church in the twenty-first century is hobbled by a lack of financial resources. It is a sign of our lack of faithfulness. Jesus never taught that we ought to tithe; he assumed it. His issue with tithing was when it was abused.

I know all the reasons why pastors don't tithe. I have used them, unfortunately. Early in my career, I rationalized that my life was ministry so tithing was unnecessary and an unwarranted burden. I have heard laypeople say that they do not tithe because they give of their time and talent. I've said that as well. These are excuses to avoid the financial discipline of tithing.

Pastors need to honestly address the idolatry of money, beginning in our own hearts and minds. Pastors do not enter ministry with the expectation that we will earn a huge salary. We expect to be appropriately compensated for the work we do, but the call to ministry is beyond the allure of finances. For some of us, that means that we struggle to make ends meet. I understand that, but tithing almost never compromises our ability to "make ends meet." Instead, it pushes us to manage what we have responsibly. Those in the congregations I have served who tithe are almost always among the most financially responsible.

That is not to say that tithing is always easy. It isn't. There have been times when I didn't want to tithe. I thought it was a limiting intrusion on already limited resources. But my faith has grown through those temptations. Faith is not always easy, and the practices of faith are not always easy either. On the other hand, faith, like a muscle, grows when there is resistance on it. Facing this temptation grows understanding and empathy within us for others who struggle with the burdens of faith.

Leaders in the twenty-first-century church should not be afraid to address the financial needs of the congregation, the biblical call to tithing, or the resistance to giving that many of our members have. When we tithe from our take-home pay, we can with integrity call upon the disciples in our churches to do the same. Disciple-making ministries grow their financial base because disciples aren't afraid of being challenged to give. The grace of God comes when we are privileged to say to someone whose circumstances have taken a tragic turn for the worse that they are freed from the obligation of tithing. I have been able to share that with wonderful people who have lost their jobs, experienced the onset of health problems, or had many other difficulties. The response has always been gratitude and the desire to give back when it became possible—and what an incredible opportunity to care for families in need.

In order to have these conversations, the pastor needs to know what people are giving. I know the giving of those in my congregation, and have never had the giving or lack of giving become an issue in the providing of pastoral care. I want to know when their practice changes, up or down, because something has happened in their lives. When I reach out to them, their giving is not the primary issue. The reason for the change is the issue. Often the most obstreperous of our members are those who give the least. This shouldn't surprise us, as those who are the most self-centered are those who will hang on to what they have and insist on their own ways. The pocketbook, as Luther noted, may be the last part of a person to be converted but it works wonders on the heart.

"Pastor Mike, I want to thank you for calling us about our change in giving," one congregation member said. "We're really sorry that we can't give more but my mother is now in nursing care and I need to support her financially."

"I think you are absolutely doing the right thing," I replied. "How can I or our Stephen Ministers be of help? Would you like us to visit your mother and give her Holy Communion?"

"No thanks, Pastor Mike," he replied. Then there was a pause and he said something I have never forgotten. "You know, Pastor Mike, you're the first one to ever call us when we have changed our giving. I just want you to know that it means a lot to us that you cared enough to notice and call."

Generosity begets generosity. Miserly ministry, likewise, creates a culture of penny pinching. I am not suggesting a lack of financial management. I am suggesting that the Christian leader in the twenty-first-century church will need to make decisions about her financial stewardship and the expectations she will have for the churches she serves. Then she can articulate the call to stewardship with an inner confidence that will help her face the reaction of those who have for decades been taught that the church doesn't really expect much financially from its members.

On the other side of the decision to practice generosity is a great deal of personal satisfaction and joy. I have never met a happy miser, but I have had the privilege of knowing the joy of generosity in many of my friends.

At St. Mark, we launched a capital drive that called for sacrificial giving. I knew that if I was going to make house calls or speak with individuals and families about such a gift, my wife and I would have to make the decision first. We prayed about it. We argued about it. We finally agreed and made our sacrificial pledge. Our conviction is that we cannot out-give God. Somehow, we believe that God will make those extraordinary gifts possible—and so far, God has!

Sacrificial giving is one more chance to exercise the risks of discipleship. Over and above our regular tithing, in addition to our usual support of the charities we give to, we are willing, for the sake of the vision of God's ministry at St. Mark, to extend ourselves and risk. If the vision was not compelling and clear, the need so great, we would not sacrifice for it—nor would I ask others to.

Personal Caregiving

I began running in 1978. I did not choose to run because it was a good idea. Frankly, I had been struggling with an undiagnosed illness for more than nine months. The physicians I had seen gave me a list of possible illnesses—all of which were frightening to a young pastor just beginning his ministry with a wife and two small children. As I tried to come to grips with my illness and its transient symptoms, I began reading about stress management. In my readings, I became convinced that regular exercise couldn't hurt. And, given the family history of cardiopulmonary disease, I began to jog. I remember after the first few runs I was spent after less than a mile. Since that inauspicious beginning, I have run a marathon, many half-marathons, and countless ten and six "Ks." On a whim, I plugged into my computer a conservative estimate of miles run over the past forty-five years. I came up with an astounding 80,000 miles!

I continue to run. I no longer run competitively. I run—actually it is a slow run or a moderate jog—for my health's sake. I recognize that eventually I will probably no longer be able to run because my knees or hips or some other part of my body will give out. Then, I'll take up bicycling or something else.

Exercise

My body simply works better and feels better when I exercise regularly. Yours will too. God has created us with a need for spiritual and physical exercise. St. Paul wrote, "Don't you know that you yourselves are God's temple and that God's Spirit dwells in your midst?" (1 Cor. 3:16 NIV) Our bodies are the temples of the Holy Spirit, and we are to treat them with respect. I believe that respect is a clarion call to regular, appropriate exercise. Part of discipleship is the care of our bodies as a discipline of stewardship.

The key is to know your body, what it will tolerate, and then simply begin. I had no interest in weight lifting, though I now know how helpful that can be for our physical well-being. I was a lifeguard during college, and the thought of swimming laps after all the ones I had to swim for that job is of no interest either. So I began to jog—and ended up running far beyond the time or distance I ever imagined. If anyone had told me that I'd run that far or for this long, I probably would never have gotten started!

You may find it helpful to find a partner or a class at the local YMCA or another fitness club to start your exercise regimen. I began with a running partner. Later, running became a solitary endeavor for me because I wanted to pray or simply shut my mind down. Do whatever will help you get started. Start easy and build up. There have been times in my life when a personal trainer was very helpful. I tend to push myself physically, and a trainer set limits that actually helped me build up to the goal I had set. I also found the trainer could encourage me so that I actually lifted more than I thought I could. Just find something that regularly works and helps you. Then, start.

Diet

Pastors are called to honor our Creator by honoring our bodies, and that includes a healthy diet. We are presently suffering from an epidemic of obesity in the United States. It is the consequence of our standard of living. While studying stress management, I learned that some of my favorite foods, like coffee (and if you are Lutheran it is a food!) were only helpful in moderation. So I began to watch my intake, only to discover that I was drinking well over twelve cups of coffee a day. No wonder my hands shook!

Moderation is also essential when it comes to alcoholic beverages. St. Paul writes: "Stop drinking only water, and use a little wine because of your stomach and your frequent illnesses" (1 Tim. 5:23 NIV). Alcohol is a friend until it isn't. The problem with alcoholic beverages is that they can mask the loneliness and isolation of the Christian leader. The temptation is to use alcohol as a self-medicating drug to help cope with changes and demands. Paying attention is the key.

There is no diet known to humankind that will eliminate death. There are diets, however, that help keep it at a distance. Diet and exercise help equip the Christian leader with the energy, health, and stamina to meet the challenges of our time. Change requires energy; leaders anticipate the changes and recognize the nutrition necessary to see them through.

Sleep

My wife is an adjunct professor at a local university. She cares about her work. She cares about her students. So, knowing that she was facing a major class and needed to relate to her students to establish a working relationship with them for their student teaching experiences, I asked what has become a standard question at the Foss household: "How did you sleep?" She told me that she had been up working on the syllabus most of the night. We laughed, because when I am preparing a significant class at church or looking toward our future, I spend most of the night awake too.

People who care about their work often find that their night's sleep is compromised. The problem is that if our sleep is consistently interrupted, our ability to think and perform is not what we expect it to be. As a result, we can make decisions that we wished we hadn't. In fact, sleep research tells us that we need a certain number of hours of sleep to clear out the detritus of our thoughts and memories. We need a number of hours of sleep, unique to each of us, in order to think clearly and organize our thoughts and decisions. The commitment to sleep is critical to the twenty-first-century leader. Without it, we will find ourselves unable to anticipate the changes we must make and interact with the people without whom our ministry is limited.

Sleep is the time when the brain and the soul recharge themselves. Slumber is not the absence of activity; it is the necessary recess for activity to be productive. The twenty-first-century church leader will recognize his or her need for sleep.

I recommend a time of devotion before sleep. This is the moment when our past is brought to the God of the present and the future. This is also the place where we can entrust our future to the One who will guide us and bring to our mind unconsidered factors and options that can help us make critical decisions. We trust Jesus Christ to take this day with all of its complications and future considerations and make of it what only he can: a blessing.

During such a time of devotion, think back on the day. What happened? Specifically, what happened that you wished you could do over? Why? What happened in the day that you can identify as the activity of the Holy Spirit? Did you meet God in the day? When and how? Then, entrust the day that has come and gone into the care and wisdom of our eternal God. This is the ever-vigilant One for whom night and day are alike. This is the One whom the psalmist describes as the Lord who watches over us, and "he who watches over Israel will neither slumber nor sleep" (Ps. 121:4 NIV). As you reflect on the day, imagine that the Savior has walked with you and touched all that you have done and all whom you have met. Can you trust him to make right what was wrong? Can you entrust to him all the difficult decisions, the critical moments of the day? Leaders reflect on and rehearse decisions we have made and those yet to be implemented. This is a core attribute of leadership, but failure to entrust our decisions to God can compromise our rest and health.

Here is a simple prayer to use during this time of devotion: "Let the night come, O Lord, and fill its darkness with your light. Remind me that you will be vigilant when I am sleeping and that my worries will be in your hands. Then, O God of night and day, let me rest confidently in you and awaken in the morning refreshed. Amen."

Faith is the bed upon which true rest and relaxation come. As a Christian leader of the twenty-first-century church, practice trusting God enough to rest in his care and promises. The outcome will be a blessing to you and your congregation.

Managing Emotions

The question is not whether we will have feelings; the only question is how we will manage them. Entrusting our feelings and responses to God's care is critical for long-term emotional health. Managing emotions is one of the significant tasks of leaders.

Feelings are neither right nor wrong; they just are. However, the judgments and actions that emerge from those feelings do have moral content.. So the first task of Christian leaders in managing emotions is to acknowledge that we have feelings—some of which are surprising!

Only as we are able to acknowledge and identify them can we begin to manage our emotions faithfully.

* * *

"I don't know what to do," he said. "I can't believe she is going." I had been called to be with him in the hospital as his wife lay dying. She had been ill for over two years. During that time, she had been in and out of the hospital and losing weight and strength, but the evening before she had a recurrence of heart problems. At the hospital, she experienced heart failure. Now, hooked up to monitors and all the apparatus necessary to keep her alive, we spoke in the hallway in hushed tones as he faced the difficult decision to remove life support. "It's what she would want," he said, his voice failing. "But I just don't know what to do."

My heart ached for him. I knew them both well. My own feelings of grief welled up within me. As I acknowledged my own emotions, I took a deep breath and put my hand on his shoulder. He turned and wept. With tears in my eyes and a deep ache in my heart, I was aware that I was less interested in being a "professional caregiver" and more in just feeling with him. All I managed to say was, "I'm so sorry."

After a moment of shared silence, he looked up and said. "OK . . . I'm ready to tell them to let her go." And that's what he did.

Leaders can experience a range of emotions. Some of them can be overwhelming, like my grief in that hospital hallway. Others can come in moments and times when it is not possible to fully experience them. Leaders are familiar with the sudden onset of anger or pain in moments when we cannot share them. Managing our feelings includes not just naming them to ourselves, but also choosing how and when we will deal with them.

I have found that postponing difficult feelings can really work. I make a grand bargain with myself: "I can't deal with or express this now. I will return to this feeling and remember the circumstances at a particular time"—and I name that time. Then, when that time comes, I find a way to be in a safe place to return to the circumstances and feeling. This practice has allowed me to face difficult people or situations and manage my response to them.

Beneath this practice is the confidence that, although I will find myself in situations beyond my control, God is still God. I can trust that there is nothing that God and I cannot handle—even when it doesn't feel like it. Our Savior knows human emotions and loves the human beings who experience them. That means I can trust him to lead me to deal with my feelings and responses to them even when they are not appropriate.

I own my feelings and my responses to them. I trust God to help me understand when I need to apologize or make amends for inappropriate actions. I also trust that God will reveal when my feelings were appropriate and my responses were healthy. Not acknowledging my feelings does not provide a healthy foundation for my emotional health. Instead, I'll find myself in bondage to forces I eventually cannot ignore.

Christian leaders must strive to both manage and learn from our emotional responses. This means that we will discover faith as truth-telling. Trusting God enough to speak the truth in love, as Scripture says, is essential for Christian leaders. Truth-telling requires faith because it is risky. We cannot control how others will react. We can only examine our motives and desired outcomes and then take the prayerful risk of sharing what is real in our perceptions.

Making Difficult Decisions

"I'm glad you are considering coming onto our staff," I said to her. "I have heard nothing but good things about your work."

"I have heard a lot about you too," she said.

"Really," I responded. "What have you heard?

"Well—I've heard that you are blunt. You tell people what you really think." She paused, and I wondered where this was going. "But I think I'll find that refreshing," she concluded with a smile.

I don't think of myself as blunt. Later, I asked her to tell me if I was ever too blunt and she agreed to do so. On the other hand, my staff and lay leaders know that they will never have to worry about where I am on any given issue. I'll tell them. I don't want them looking over their shoulders and wondering!

Neither do I want to do any harm. Twelve-step programs speak about making amends with those we have hurt *unless it will do further harm to them.* That is good advice when it comes to truth-telling. I want to speak the truth unless my motive is just to lash out or get back at someone. That's the time to deal with my own feelings and needs, not speak to someone else about their behaviors or attitudes. But if we do not speak the hard truth to others, they will often be blindsided by decisions that we must make. Speaking the truth is always about providing a realistic assessment of the situation and what choices are really available. Pretending that unrealistic options are available in order to be nice is destructive. It suggests a future that is not possible. Caring about the other person enough to tell the truth is an essential commitment for authentic leadership.

That means leaders will not please everyone. Most of us in the Christian church desire to make others happy. There's nothing wrong with that as long as we understand that it cannot be done all the time. There will be moments when leaders need to address issues and make decisions that will leave some unhappy or dissatisfied. The goal is not to intentionally alienate people. The goal is to make the right decision at the right time. Others will have legitimate disagreements with us—and some not so legitimate—but not deciding or acting will not please everyone either.

Effective Christian leadership for the twenty-first century seeks to build consensus but will make decisions when consensus cannot be achieved. This requires a consultative leadership style. The opinions of those most affected by a decision must be sought out. The perspectives of those who will be directly involved in the implementation of the decision need to be discovered as well. But if consensus cannot be reached and the leader believes a decision must be made, then she will need to make it.

How do leaders experience inner peace when we need to make a decision that we know others will neither approve of nor feel good about? Two keys can help in these circumstances. First, we ask ourselves if the consultative process was fully operational. Were those to be affected invited into the conversation? Have we understood and acknowledged not only the opinions but the feelings of others to the best of our ability? If the process proves healthy, then we can move to the second key.

The second key to bring peace after a difficult decision is to wait and watch to see how the decision is implemented. Sometimes, as the decision rolls out, we will learn that the best process nonetheless led us to a bad decision. The only thing to do in those circumstances is admit mistakes and work to limit the damage. If a leader is willing to acknowledge mistakes, my experience is that the disciple/members of the congregation are willing to forgive and help move the ministry in a positive direction. Authentic leadership emerges when leaders are willing to be human and own our mistakes.

3

The Pastor's Vision

The pastor's inner foundation, discussed in the previous chapter, becomes the platform for effective ministry with the people of God. Faithful and fruitful ministry in the twenty-first century will call for vision, mission, and culture formation within the congregation. The vision is the destination, the end toward which a ministry is directed. The strategy for achieving that vision is the people in mission. Such a dynamic process will require respectful listening as well as clear articulation. A clear vision will inspire energy and effort in those who choose to follow. The result will be that the vision will become greater and deeper, and both leader and followers will experience significance and joy.

Twenty-first-century churches look to their leaders for vision. Vision does not emerge from a people but is shared from the leader to the people. Once the leader has shared the vision with the people, they decide whether they will follow the vision. If the people adopt the vision, then it will grow larger than the leader's vision and embrace more people to accomplish more than expected.

Acts 16 gives us an example of a compelling vision. Having been frustrated by the Holy Spirit's denial of their entry into the center of the Roman province of Asia Minor (present-day Turkey), St. Paul and his companions have ended up on the coast at Troas. During the night, he has a vision of a Macedonian man pleading for him to come and declare the gospel to him. Upon awakening, Paul shares his vision with his companions. Compelled to follow that vision, they sail across the strait to Macedonia as soon as possible. The result was a unified purpose that proved to be perhaps the most successful of all St. Paul's missionary endeavors—see 2 Corinthians 8.

The elements of the narrative in Acts 16 are helpful. First, Paul and his companions make the journey into Asia Minor only to be frustrated in their attempts to go where they thought they should. Second, this frustration continues until they are led to Troas, a location they had no intention of going. Only then does Paul receive the vision and the call. Lastly, we see that the vision is clear and compelling: they know where they ought to go and that the need is great.

Using this as a biblical template for vision we learn that, first, vision is born of frustration. Satisfied individuals are not open to a vision. Vision requires dissatisfaction with the status quo and, therefore, is always a call to change. Satisfaction resists change and sees no need for a new future, but frustration is God's doorway to the future. Frustration creates the desire for a new possibility that, in turn, opens the heart and mind to vision.

Second, finding ourselves in a place we didn't expect often opens us to new possibilities and vision. God often acts to bring us to a place where the vision can be implemented. Troas was the closest port to Macedonia. By ending up there, Paul and his entourage were in the perfect place to execute the vision sent them.

Third, a vision is clear and specific. The man in Paul's dream was a Macedonian man. His plea was desperate. The destination and purpose of the vision were, therefore, clear.

Lastly, followers endorse a vision. Paul's companions join him in crossing the strait and entering into uncharted territory for them in the confidence that this was God's call. Their vision was an extension of their shared mission.

Twenty-first century vision will often include the elements discussed above. The pastor will need to experience a sense of frustration and dissatisfaction with the current state of her ministry. This can lead to prayerful seeking of God's future for her and the people she serves. The vision for ministry can often be accessed by simply asking, "If you could picture your ministry or congregation in five years as a vibrant community of faith fulfilling the calling of God to them, what would that look like?"

Soul Sight

God has created in the heart of pastors and lay leaders a deep desire to be effective. Effective ministry is both faithful and fruitful. Vision is the expression of our desire to be fruitful. As such, Christian vision is soul sight. Christian vision for the congregation is our attempt at catching a glimpse of God's dream for our ministry and our church. Without this heartfelt prayer, the church succumbs to the banal, going through the motions of maintenance without passion.

With all the Protestant congregations across this country going out of business, if your church is still standing, God has a purpose for that church in its place and time. This may be to join with another congregation in ministry. It may be to radically reframe your shared understanding of what the congregation is about. But it is always God's desire that his church be alive and serving the needs of its disciples and the community and world in which it is placed. Anything less is simply unworthy of the God we worship. Yet so many pastors and congregations seem willing to accept that.

Perhaps, there was a time when that was sufficient. Twenty-first-century leaders know that time has passed.

When a leader catches sight of a vision, it must be large enough to require a multitude of others to achieve. Otherwise, it is simply a personal dream. The vision should, therefore, be thought of as a very large umbrella under which many smaller umbrellas can be embraced. These smaller umbrellas are the specific visions of those with whom we work and serve. Therefore, a vision for disciple-making ministry would be large enough to encourage specific visions for disciple-making youth ministry, disciple-making children's ministry, disciple-making small groups, etc. These various ministries grow out of the passions of others within the congregation but serve to advance the larger vision by incorporating it in a specific expression. Those visions that do not advance the larger vision must be set aside as inappropriate at this time for the work of the congregation.

Here is an example of how this works. A woman in our congregation came to me and said, "Pastor Mike, we have two buildings that are separated by a parking lot. We are not a unified campus. So, we'd like to ask your permission to purchase some large flower containers with the St. Mark logo prominently displayed on them. If we have them at the entries to both our buildings, we think we'll begin to forge a single identity for this campus." She paused and then said, "Here's the design we'd like to have—and it won't cost the church anything because we'll raise the money for it ourselves. Can we go ahead?"

I was taken aback. The vision for a unified campus as a center for disciple-making ministry was part of the emerging vision of St. Mark. This group of women, which included master gardeners, had independently come up with a way to bring that closer to reality—and it wasn't going to tax our already-stretched budget!

If you visit St. Mark today, you'll see these large containers with our logo at the entrances to both our Worship Center and our Discipleship Center. The larger vision for a disciple-making ministry that grew to include two buildings embraced a smaller vision for landscaping that brought a unifying factor to our buildings and grounds that I would never have thought about.

Another example of this was in our youth ministry. The decision to take our youth on a mission trip among the Amish was not my idea. Frankly, I tried to discourage it. But when our youth leader justified it by saying that it would encourage our kids to get "unplugged" and focus on their own discipleship, I was challenged by a unique smaller vision that could significantly advance our larger vision as a congregation. The trip turned out to have an incredible impact on the spiritual lives of our youth. Many of them came back and shared their faith with their parents in a way they never had before.

The vision of the pastor is not complete in and of itself. Rather, it is the arena within which others can share and implement their dreams and the call of God as they understand it. Nonetheless, the larger vision should be clear.

Dreaming God's Dream for Your Ministry and Church

"We will welcome any and all who come to St. Mark," I shared in a recent sermon, "whether they are unchurched, dechurched, or looking from another congregation. We are not seeking people from other congregations—in fact, we pray that they will feel the call to stay and energize their own church. But if they are looking, we will welcome them here." I watched as the congregation took in my words. Then I continued: "The point is that we are here to make disciples of Jesus Christ: followers of the Savior who strive to practice and live their faith. And we cannot make disciples if we deny others access to Christ's church. We are not here to set up barriers but to welcome anyone who seeks to meet the Lord Jesus Christ here. Then, by the power of the Holy Spirit, we will do our best to help them grow deeper in faith."

St. Mark is a warm congregation. We have people who consistently seek out those who they do not know to greet them and welcome them to worship. Sometimes this leads to an interesting meeting of one member/disciple with another because we are too large for everyone to know everyone else. But they still reach out and take that risk.

This is not the experience of other churches. At the church of a pastoral friend, no one reached out to welcome or even acknowledge me as we waited for worship to begin—though it was clear that I was a visitor. If I hadn't known better, I would have thought that those around us thought they were better than we were—which, interestingly enough, is exactly what polls tell us those outside the church think we think.

Discipleship moves beyond membership as a focus for ministry. The goal is not simply to get people onto our rolls. The prayed-for and desired outcome is that individuals and families grow deeper in their faith. This is demonstrated in a number of visible behaviors. People will talk about their faith more often. There will be a desire for more Bible studies. Families make time for worship as a top priority. Financial resources, the gifts and talents of those within the congregation, are more freely shared.

The vision for disciple-making ministry is not anti-institutional. It is, rather, pre-institutional. That is to say that the value of people is in their relationship with God. The church serves that purpose. And the result is counterintuitive: when the church serves the spiritual needs of people, they, in turn, desire to serve the needs of the church. When the needs of the congregation are primary, people opt out because they feel used. When the call is to meet Jesus Christ, grow in faith, and from that faith change the world, the church is fulfilling its mission through the lives of its member/discipless.

The activities of the congregation are, therefore, not limited by what has been done. Instead, any activity that advances the congregation's mission and vision can pay for itself (or help grow the giving to pay for itself) and can gather enough interest to have the necessary people power to get the job done. Ministry is not limited, but becomes an unlimited expression of the vision of the congregation.

Sharing the Dream

That means that the vision needs to be clearly communicated so that the member/discipless of the church can enroll in it. People enroll in the vision when they can articulate that vision and give expression to it through their faith and service within and beyond the congregation.

"I don't know how to make disciples of Jesus Christ," one woman said in frustration. "I mean, I believe in it, but I'm not a pastor or even trained in the Bible. I can't do it!"

"But aren't you a den mother for your son's Cub Scout troop?" I asked.

"Well, yes I am. But I don't see how that fits," she responded.

"When you are with those boys, don't you try to grow them as ethical persons no matter what their faith might be? And," I persisted, "isn't that a part of how you live your faith with your son?"

She smiled and said, "I never thought of it that way. But you're right—my son and I often talk about how being a Christian fits with scouting and means that we respect any boy's position on faith." Then she laughed as she continued, "Well, I guess I'm helping at least one boy grow in discipleship, and that's my son!"

The power of our people to live their vision outside of church life is often overlooked. That woman had not consciously made the connection between her life of faith and the work she did with her son and the other scouts. But it was there. She only had to make the connection. We have too long thought of ministry as happening only at church. Ministries that help connect people's lives to their faith encourage a wonderful alignment, first, of the various ministries within the congregation and, secondly, of the everyday lives of our people.

Our member/discipless are the missionaries of the twenty-first century. Pastors—once considered front-line evangelists in our society—now must step back and equip the laity for this ministry of witness. There are at least three reasons for this. First, there is a tragic distrust of leaders—including pastors—in our society today. Leaders are viewed initially with skepticism. Pastors are often met with a cynicism about faith. It may be unconscious and unexpressed, but we know it when we experience it. Our witness of faith is discounted because we are pastors.

Second, our laypeople will be involved in conversations and invited to places we will never go. They will be involved in the conversation with a coworker about a family member who is undergoing chemotherapy for cancer—a conversation that might never happen in church. They will be invited to the cocktail party where they will hear about a neighbor's infidelity and prayers and help can be given. These are the points of contact that pastoral leaders will need to equip their disciples for. This is where real faith meets real life.

Third, the deep desire of our time is for an authentic faith. When our people are living their faith as real people—as opposed to the perfectionistic Christian so often caricatured in movies, on television, and in literature—the Holy Spirit often touches the lives of others in the depths of their hungry souls. This is particularly significant given our increasingly secular society. Christian leaders in the twenty-first century neither accept this increased secularization as unavoidable nor do we accept the caricature of the judgmental, rigid churchgoer.

A Vision for Team Ministry

When the vision for discipleship has been shared, adopted by the congregation, and has entered into the active lives of the people of God, the church grows and the need for an effective staff ministry emerges. I believe that passionate team ministry will shape effective churches for the future.

Jim Collins, in his book *Built to Last*, talks about the tasks of the leader of a visionary company. Among them, he tells us, is getting the right people on the bus and then the right people in the right seat on the bus. Creating an effective team is an evolving skill. That is to say, as the church changes, the needs for staff change. Not all people are able to adjust their gifts to the changing circumstances of the congregation, no matter how gifted they may be. Vibrant churches are changing churches. They will go through stages based upon the worship attendance at all regularly scheduled worship services. The larger the average attendance, the more specific will be the needs for an effective staff. The smaller the church, the greater will be the need for generalists. The shift from generalists on staff to specialists is both complicated and difficult to master. The key is to have a clear set of stated values and a clear and often-repeated mission and vision statement. These will be established upon a clear, shared set of beliefs that include an openly stated view of the authority of Scripture.

At St. Mark, we have published statements of our core values, vision, and mission. This has allowed us to hold ourselves and our growing variety of ministries accountable to our stated self-identity.

It is no longer sufficient to be affiliated with a particular denomination as an indicator of self-identity. In the Evangelical Lutheran Church in America, for example, we have congregations and clergy whose views of Scripture can be either high or low. We have those who see themselves as conservative, while others, of the same denomination, see themselves as more progressive. We have some who characterize themselves as Confessional Lutheran, while others place themselves in the "evangelical" arena of Protestantism. When people visit our churches, one of the things they are looking for is clear identification of where the congregation stands on biblical or social issues. Such clarity is not only helpful to those who visit; it is helpful to the member/disciples within that congregation.

This clarity sets the direction and expectations of staff. I have watched as capable pastors and staff members have slipped into dysfunction because they functionally disagreed about one or more core identification indicators. If the pastor, for example, is deeply committed to the call to personal discipleship but then hires a staff member whose commitments are to social justice—with or without such personal discipleship—sooner or later there will be a conflict of core visions. Unfortunately, most of these conflicts leak out into the congregation no matter how much the parties involved try to keep them to themselves. An effective staff is committed to a set of clearly identified core values and a shared vision. If one staff member is committed to the membership model while the congregation is moving towards discipleship, that member will find himself blocking ministry growth unintentionally. In cases like these, it is necessary to make the difficult decision to ask a staff member off the bus. Care should be given to identify the causes and help the person make the transition whenever possible. But a conflict of vision or core values cannot be negotiated. Both may be right; they just can't both be right in the same context at the same time.

In developing a staffing plan, build upon growth. If children's ministry is growing, staff to continue and expand that growth. Staffing to compensate for a perceived weakness where growth is not happening or where the need is only internally identified is almost always a mistake.

I was once asked to consult with a local church as they began to re-vision their ministry. As an older congregation, they had traditional worship as their centerpiece. Now they wanted to call a young pastor to reach out to the community though the neighborhood was aging and declining. "What we really want," they said, "is an associate pastor who can reach out to the young people of our community." The problem was that they had no basis for such a ministry except their hope that young people would come and save their church.

"What if," I said, "the new pastor is successful and young people begin to attend your church and they wanted a contemporary worship service?" There was a stunned silence. Then one of the members said, "Well, I guess if that's the only way we could keep them, we'd let them have it." To which another member of the team replied, "As long as it isn't at 10 o'clock on Sunday morning. That's my service, and I like the organ!"

The first assumption was that change could occur without disrupting the present schedule and practice of the congregation. The second assumption was that any younger pastor would be effective in reaching out to younger people. Neither assumption was accurate. The truth was that the church was in a declining urban area that was, simultaneously, growing older. Staffing for younger people to come to their church was probably not going to work. However, staffing a parish nurse for the community would be a great outreach strategy. Such a position would not only build upon the strength of that church but also meet the needs of their neighborhood.

As the congregation grows, it will go through changes that will require adjusting the staffing plan. Whether it's for outreach, as in the case above, or for internal ministry effectiveness, the single determining factor is where the need is demonstrated by growth. Structure your staff for building upon growth, or invest in the clear potential for growth in your area. Then develop both a clear job description and set of expectations. If it is an investment for potential growth, then adopt a "sunset clause" for when the ministry will be terminated if expectations aren't met. Finally, call someone who is in agreement with the culture of the congregation or the culture the congregation is moving to become.

Staffing for change requires projecting the best of the culture of the congregation forward in time. This is always risky but the risk is minimized when the staff position(s) created express both a agreement with the present culture and embody the best hopes of that ministry for a vibrant future. Even with these factors clearly articulated, mistakes can be made. So, in the spirit of adventure so necessary in our time of ministry, on-going assessments are essential. What is assessed and how the success of any such venture is determined ought to be identified before the staffing decision is made. The calling, for example, of a parish nurse rather than a young associate pastor should be based upon the ministry needs identified. The job description will need to identify if outreach is a part of that job description and, if so, how it will be measured and achieved. Otherwise, the judgment on the effectiveness of that ministry will degenerate into the sentimentality of whether we like that person or not. This is neither fair nor adequate for either the candidate selected or the congregation to which the candidate comes to serve.

It is important to reiterate that growth is an outcome, not a goal. When needs are met, whether physical, spiritual or emotional, growth often occurs. When growth is the goal, the strategies for staffing will almost always fall short of the hopes and dreams of the congregation because reaching out is for the sake of those already present. The assumption is that if it is meaningful to those already present in the church then it will (or ought to be) meaningful to others – whether they know it or not!

4

The Church's Environment

How people outside the church see the church will shape their idea of what that congregation is like. If the physical appearance of the buildings is worn and the inside cluttered, those who come to that church will make judgments about the congregation—for example, that the congregation is in decline or unable to pay the bills necessary to make the property attractive. These assumptions may not be accurate at all, but the perception is the reality for people outside the church. We need to look with "outside eyes" at how we present ourselves to the community at large, so we can begin to produce a physical environment that more accurately represents the vitality of the congregation.

The exterior of the church both reflects and reinforces the interior personality and culture of the congregation. When the people of God match the attractive presentation of the church building with warmth and healthy boundaries, the authenticity of the congregation is established.

The Physical Environment

I drove by the church and couldn't help but notice the sign in the front yard. It was awful: paint was peeling, the lettering was a faded

"Welcome," and the name of the congregation was unreadable. The impression was of a church that was long past caring about how anyone outside of the membership thought of them. I wondered if the inside of the church building was as worn out as that sign, and prayed that God would have mercy on them and bless them with new vision and hope. Later, I learned that the congregation was disbanding and hoped to sell their property.

Churches only get one shot at a good first impression. When people are looking for a church to visit, they pay attention to the outward appearance of the property and grounds as an indicator of the internal spiritual health of the congregation. That is not always a fair representation, but it is reality nonetheless. Christian leaders must pay attention to the message we are sending at the curb of our property.

At St. Mark, we have a new sign on the main street by our property. The old sign, now placed on a side street, is weathered and worn. Since we are in the process of capital construction and remodeling, I have chosen not to fight the "old guard" for whom that sign has nostalgic symbolism. When the reconstruction of our worship center begins, we will have to remove that sign. Not much traffic passes along that street, but if anyone is looking to visit a church and drives by St. Mark, I hope they do so where our new sign stands.

The issue is not simply the appearance of our property. It is whether we believe that God is calling us to reach out to the community as a welcome center for the love of God in Jesus Christ. If so, then we need to do all we can to present ourselves as a welcoming church.

The church of Jesus Christ is worth our very best. When I came to St. Mark, we collected clothing and foodstuffs at the entrance to our sanctuary. We habitually used old card tables, with worn corners and shaky legs, for sign-up sheets for our ministries. As I walked through the building with our then-administrator, Maxine Bruinekool, we agreed that we needed to de-clutter our worship space. Together, we went through the entire building moving bags and old card tables. As we took time for a cup of coffee, Maxine laughed: "I can't tell you how long I've wanted to do this! The best of who we are as a congregation has been lost in all this stuff!"

But later, I heard from those who were unhappy about our actions. "What have you done?" one angry member asked. "I've always liked that we could see where to drop our clothes. Now, we have to take it to the Fellowship Hall. And what about our sign-up sheets? Who will know where to find them?"

No matter how I tried to help her understand that people needed to worship in a building that was similar in appearance to their places of work or their homes, I could never justify our efforts. I was sad when she chose to leave the church.

The cleaning of the worship center was symbolic of the emotional cleansing of our congregation. We would no longer be a church that accepted whatever anyone offered, whether it was helpful or not. We would be a church with emotional boundaries. The standard for care and behavior would be based upon what was good and helpful, what was in keeping with our efforts to share the good news of Jesus with our world.

If we care, as Christian leaders, about the condition of our buildings, our efforts will necessarily collide with those who don't want any change. I understand that. But the church has for far too long been held hostage by the few who resist change. Frankly, there are no major institutions in our society that haven't undergone significant change. Ask your local physician or banker and they'll give you a chronicle of changes, few of which they wanted. In the Christian church, we are called to speak the gospel into our age—and we speak into a society and time of change and hope. De-clutter your church—not just because it is a good idea, but because unless you do, many will simply bypass your congregation for another that presents itself in keeping with their expectations and needs.

What we are talking about is not unlike Jesus clearing the money changers from the temple. The issue is sacred space. Sacred space is that place where we can empty ourselves, come before the God who alone is God, and be refreshed. We need sacred spaces, and simplicity demands that we de-clutter them.

At St. Mark, we open our worship center for prayer any time anyone desires to find a place to pray. I am among them. The empty altar, vacant pews, and stained-glass windows invite me away from the pressures of the world, my job, and sins. I am amazed at how many join me on a weekly basis to just be in the presence of God. Any church can make this sacred space available. Just remove the barriers and clutter that get in the way.

The Emotional Environment

When I came to St. Mark, there was an active Stephen's Ministry team in place. Shortly after my arrival, we met in my office to discuss their future. They were worried that I would not value their gifts and that I would insist on being the primary if not sole provider of pastoral care. I assured them that would not be the case. Since that conversation, their ministry has grown. Not only that, their ministry has proven to be a model for how the entire church can be the communion of saints for one another.

That meeting with the Stephen's Ministry team was the first of many that would be an intentional effort on my part to build trust within the congregation. I was blessed with the leadership of a previous pastor who had strategically healed and improved the mental and spiritual health of our congregation. But I knew that I would have to open my heart and mind to the leadership if we would share a vision of where God was calling us.

Trust is the currency of ministry. Not money. Not people. Trust. When there is a shared trust in the leadership of a congregation, the money and time of the member/disciples will necessarily follow. A leadership question that I constantly ask myself and others is, How is the trust account at St. Mark? The answer will tell me what needs tending and how we can do it.

How do you invest in the "trust account" of your ministry? One of the most important ways is to close the communication loop. When we take an offering for a special project, we report back on the outcome as soon as possible. When a member/disciple of our congregation e-mails or phones in a request, we try to reply as quickly as possible, preferably within twenty-four hours, even if it is to say that we cannot answer the question yet. Then we explain why. When we make a mistake, we own it and tell the church about it. This is not always possible, but delayed responses and unclear messages that leave the church or its member/disciples confused or anxious are all withdrawals from the trust account. Failure to respond in a timely manner to phone calls or e-mails will often be experienced by the sender as a dismissal.

This doesn't mean that there will not be some e-mails or phone calls that we will choose to set aside or ignore. When someone wants to engage in a conversation in order to sell something or uses communication in an in appropriate way, we can choose to ignore them. The difference is that we consciously make the decision by weighing the contact and its potential impact on the trust account.

E-mail responses should be carefully considered. The problem with an e-mail in an emotionally loaded situation is that it is almost always read much more harshly than the writer intended. We cannot put the communication within the context of body language or voice inflection. In simple matters, an e-mail response is appropriate. But when there is potential conflict or the situation is emotionally loaded for any reason, a phone call or face-to-face communication is always better.

Open leaders forge open systems. Leaders who fail to communicate will unintentionally create the expectation that information can or will be withheld. This, in turn, will shape the behaviors of those involved in the ministry. The result will be distrust, anxiety, and often anger.

We entered a black hole of communication as we wrestled with the issues surrounding our building plans. First, the leaders struggled with how much debt St. Mark should take on. Then, the lending practices of banks were tightened up and what we thought we could borrow was no longer available to us. That meant that we had to rethink our plans. Our priorities remained the same, but we now had to go back to the drawing board. The consequence of these delays was an inability to identify a specific response to the congregation that would keep them informed. So we wrestled with the issues in leadership. Finally, realizing the anxiety and confusion in the congregation, we crafted and shared an appropriate message. The result was an almost immediate sense of relief in the congregation. The momentum lost during that season of struggle in leadership later began to return. And, once the explanation was given for why the congregation didn't know what was happening, the vast majority of our member/disciples accepted the explanation and trust was not significantly damaged.

These events happen in ministry. Leaders will need to be as open about the issues as possible—often in response to questions raised by individuals. Then, as soon as clarity is found, communication needs to occur. And confusing communication is actually worse than no communication.

The Spiritual Environment

"Pastor, I heard your prayer for Jack and knew it was our Jack Smith. What's he in the hospital for?" she asked.

We have prayer cards in the racks on our chairs and pews. We invite people to write prayer requests, then we collect them and they become the prayers of the people in worship. We will almost always edit any personal or confidential information when we pray. The person asking had made an identification that was not specific in our prayers, but she was right. However, unless the medical information is clearly public, we cannot divulge it.

"I'm sorry I can't say," I replied. "But thank you for caring about him. He could use your prayers."

Communication to the congregation has boundaries. Medical information is one of them. Another is related to personnel actions. If staff members leave their position for any reason other than one they choose to make public, conversation with member/disciples must be limited. This is especially true when a staff member is terminated for any reason. People want to know why. Given the personal nature of the information, we cannot tell them, either in public or private conversation.

Some in the congregation will never understand or accept this. Nonetheless, leaders know that this is privileged information and must be treated as such. When we do this, we are embedding our theology in the psyche of the congregation. The "golden rule" shapes how and what we say about others, whether it is a medical condition or a staff issue. If the leader has any doubt or question about whether the information requested should be shared, she shouldn't share it. This isn't hiding anything from the congregation; it is simply respecting the person involved by treating the information about them respectfully.

Christian leaders in the twenty-first-century church also know the truth of Jesus' teaching: "For there is nothing hidden that will not be disclosed, and nothing concealed that will not be known or brought out into the open" (Luke 8:17 NIV). Even when we cannot share the information or pertinent facts, we have a litmus test of doing nothing that can't "see the light of day." Leaders assume that eventually the information will come out. In the meantime, we test our actions and information so that, when it becomes known, we will have shown an appropriate handling of the situation. If we cannot have confidence in that, then we will need to take action to rectify the situation as best we can.

Just as our Lord took seriously the emotional state of those with whom he interacted, the Christian leader should affirm the emotional realities of the congregation and its individual member/disciples. Simply responding to the feelings present is often all that is necessary in order to then take the appropriate action or to point to the promises of God. Acknowledging the emotional content of a situation is not the same as allowing that to determine the action necessary. The woman who asked for the information on the medical condition of "Jack" cared about him. That very real concern did not, however, justify the sharing of private information.

We should reinforce our theology by how we behave. Christian leaders in the twenty-first-century church should strive to align our systems and actions so that they reflect our discipleship. In doing so, we establish an integrity that can be identified throughout the ministry of the congregation. This is new thinking. Historically, we did not have to reflect on how our theology shaped our systems and actions because, in part, they reflected the broader Judeo-Christian ethic of our culture. In a pluralistic society, this is no longer the case. Our systems, behaviors, and attitudes must be held to a higher standard than the broader cultural norms.

We therefore need to make the spiritual life and message of our ministries more visible than ever before. Many in our society no longer share the assumption that our congregations are fundamentally spiritual organizations. They often view the church as a club with a particular set of stated beliefs that, at best, help people.

Apart from worship itself, the first visible activity in making the spiritual nature of our congregations visible is the establishing of and communication about a prayer team. When we implemented the prayer cards at St. Mark, we told people that their prayers would be shared in worship and, through the coming week, with a prayer team who would lift up their prayer requests. This prayer team continues to be a foundational demonstration of our commitment to the spiritual exercises of the church beyond worship.

We have also initiated prayers for healing once a month. On the second weekend of the month, when people come forward to receive the Lord's Supper, they are invited to step to one of two prayer stations so that they may be anointed with oil and prayers may be said for them. The response has been remarkable. We have had small children (with their parents' encouragement), young people, families, and our older member/disciples step forward and ask for the anointing with oil and prayer. Again, this becomes a visible sign of the spiritual nature and commitment of the congregation.

For many of us, this conversation will seem redundant. We know that at the heart of what we do as a church is the spiritual work of the gospel. But as our society has continued to move in a secular and pluralistic direction, those outside of the church—and, unfortunately, many in the church—no longer assume that this is the case. Twenty-first-century ministry should make the heart of what we do a demonstration of the spiritual work of the Christian church.

I had just finished a five-part sermon series on prayer when I greeted Steve after worship. I knew he had been there for every one of those sermons, so I asked, "What did you think of the series on prayer? I don't think you missed one of them." He smiled and replied, "I loved them. The only problem, Pastor Mike, is that I learned a lot about prayer but I still don't know how to pray."

Discipleship translates ideas into practice. I thought a great deal about that exchange after worship and became convinced that he was right. I had talked a lot about prayer, assuming that people knew how and when to pray. That assumption was wrong. I now know that pastors and Christian leaders need to "connect the dots" between our knowledge about faith and how we put that faith into action in our lives. The truth is that if you are under the age of sixty-five, it is likely that you have never seen or heard prayer except as a table grace or by some official or pastor at an event or worship service. The prayers of these officials are usually highly stylized and do not reflect the language of everyday living. Prayer is seen as a formal, technical language or a perfunctory word at mealtime.

One of the central tasks of twenty-first-century Christian leaders is to apply faith to life. This means helping people by giving examples and challenges for them to live their faith—not just think the faith. The prayer cards we use in worship provide an opportunity to pray in the everyday language of the people in worship. This models how we can approach God without formal training or a stylized form and language. Other aspects of faith will need similar demonstration.

One of our stewardship drives took this idea and tried to place financial stewardship within the broader context of the life of faith. We proposed a Ten-Ten-Ten response: ten minutes a day in Bible reading and prayer; ten hours a month in service within or outside of St. Mark; and ten percent of take-home pay for the ministry of Christ's church. Ten minutes a day in Bible reading and prayer may not sound like much, but it is a place to begin these disciplines. It isn't threatening but, for most people, doable. That's the point: we want people to begin because we have confidence that the Holy Spirit will help them grow in the time and depth of their reading and praying. Ten hours of service a month is also achievable. The encouragement is to move from thinking about our faith to living it by applying our theology to our lives. I had a delightful conversation with a man who thought that ten hours of service was too much until I asked him how many hours a week he coached his son's team, pointing out that his faith and the ethics of his faith were demonstrably present in those sessions. Suddenly he discovered that, not only was he giving more than ten hours a month in serving, but his coaching was connected to his life of faith. Later, he told me that connection caused him to change the attitude that he took into practice.

I also try to make the application in sermons. At the end of most of my messages, I issue a challenge for the hearer to take into the week. For example, when talking about caring for others I will suggest that they pay attention to their neighbors and, if the lawn needs mowing or leaves raking, they simply offer to do it. If they learn of a neighbor living through a difficult or tragic time, I'll ask them to take a casserole to her. If a coworker shares a struggle, offer to pray for him. Or better still, if it is appropriate, pray with him then.

In one message, I was discussing St. Paul's call to patience in life. I challenged the children or young people to take time to really listen to their parents; I urged parents to engage their children in conversation to and from activities or, better yet, to find a one-on-one time with each child to check in with them. I urged those who did not have children to give way in traffic to that driver that needs to change lanes or is barging in from an on-ramp. I have had countless people tell me that they especially like the challenge in the message and work to achieve it in the coming week.

Sermon outlines provide another application. On the front of our worship bulletins is a "fill in the blank" outline. At first I thought this was simplistic and couldn't believe it would be acceptable to my listeners. What I found was that many filled them in (they still do!) and took them home to place on their kitchen counters or on their refrigerators. These people would look at the outline throughout the week. Others took the outlines and put them in their Bibles at the place of the Scripture text. I learned that many had built a book of outlines as helps in their own Bible reading.

Disciples don't leave their faith in church. Disciples know no boundary between faith and life. Faith is present to intrude when temptation comes, and comfort when difficulties arise.

Twenty-first-century Christian leaders must find ways for our people to take the conversation of worship into the home. Families are the faith forums of our time. When parents and children can talk about Jesus freely at home, they'll find it a natural topic of conversation with their friends and classmates. If faith is part of the fabric of the family, the moral contents of our faith will simply be a part of how people live.

Discipleship shapes how we live. Theology forms how we think. When the two are naturally together, we have a resilient and lived faith. This is the goal of twenty-first-century pastors and church leaders. We are not playing church. We strive to be the church.

5

The Ministry of the People

The priesthood of all believers is more than a theological idea. Opening the church to new ideas and ministries within the identifiable vision and mission of the congregation enlivens the church.

In this chapter, I invite the reader to envision and then work toward a congregation that is permission-giving in ministry, not permission-withholding.

Appropriate and healthy boundaries can be established and exercised in a permission-giving ministry. These are made clear through specific expectations and a system of accountability.

Calling, Equipping, and Commissioning God's People

We read in the Letter to the Ephesians, "The gifts [Christ] gave were that some would be apostles, some prophets, some evangelists, some pastors and teachers, to equip the saints for the work of ministry, for building up the body of Christ " (4:11-12). The purpose of gifted leaders in the church is to prepare the people of God for the works (service) of faith. The role of the pastor and Christian leader is, therefore, to call, equip, and commission the people of God for ministry. This is the vision for twenty-first-century congregational life. The focus of worship is God. The focus of our ministries is to reach and extend this vision of the church through our people.

Tim Florer is a gifted photographer. I invited him to share his work with the church, and then asked if he would form a team for the display of visual art in our church. Tim and I then recruited Brad and Caroline Reece, who own a gallery in Des Moines that features the work of his father, Maynard Reece. Together, Tim and the Reeces created a team of supporters that transformed our Discipleship Center into one of the finest venues for the visual arts in the city. Opening nights featured wine, cheese, and time with the artists, and were open to the public. We usually had two hundred or more in attendance, with about twenty from St. Mark. It was a wonderful outreach.

I had little or nothing to do with this great ministry. In fact, because the openings were on my day off, I wasn't able to attend all of them—and no one expected me to! This was a ministry inspired, created and enhanced by Tim, Brad, and Caroline with their team. If there were questions, Tim would usually check in with me, but otherwise they were equipped with a clear understanding of what was needed. In a very real way, they helped put St. Mark on the map in the greater Des Moines area.

The Christian church has always appreciated the spiritual value of art, whether it is the work of an unknown artist who drew the Orante on the walls of the catacombs in Rome, Michelangelo's Pietà, or a local artist in Des Moines. What was needed for a gallery to work at St. Mark was a team that included artists and a capable visionary who could put it all together. I am not an artist, but my vision was broad enough to allow a specific vision to emerge through a gifted member/disciple like Tim or Brad. Their clear understanding of the purpose of a gallery as community service and outreach caught the attention and led to the investment of nearly thirty other couples and individuals. This gallery was self-supporting, created a team, fit our values, vision, and mission, and accomplished its goal. But when it was decided that we needed that space for our growing children's ministry, Tim agreed. The gallery suspended its activity until we can create a new, equally attractive space, which we hope to accomplish soon.

The mission of the church belongs to the people of God. But that mission will need to be connected to the gifts and passions of people, as the possibility of a gallery connected with the gifts and passions of Tim, Brad, and Caroline. Then, the mission grew larger and with a higher quality than I had ever imagined. Nevertheless, when that ministry was impeding the growth of a core ministry of the congregation, it ended.

There were several leadership keys in this process. First, a vision was created that was large enough to include the specific visions of others. Second, that vision was connected to a gifted and passionate member/disciple. Third, that vision grew over time to require the help of others. Fourth, the vision went public with a retrospective of Maynard Reece's exceptional work. Fifth, the team grew with the involvement and financial support of others. The real mission was to serve the community and be an outreach from St. Mark, and there was ongoing accountability of the gallery to its mission. That mission was achieved as the original vision grew in scope and quality as others owned it and then shaped it.

Often, the problem in our congregations is that when we have a task that needs doing, we recruit someone to do the work without connecting that task to the gifts and passion of the person. More than that, many of our tasks are not obviously tied to the values, vision, and mission of the congregation. As a consequence, many of our member/disciples do not feel the value of their work. One of the duties of the pastor or leader is to make the connection for them. When the one who mows the lawn understands that an attractive exterior is inviting to others and witnesses to the quality of the church's ministry, keeping the lawn neat and trim suddenly has higher value—and it will show!

Use simple service opportunities to discover the gifts and passions of church member/disciples. If a person is willing to fill an immediate need, observe how they go about it. Then, dialogue with them about what was accomplished to discern if activities like that are a good fit for them. This identifies gifts and passions. The next opportunity to serve ought to be in line with what you have learned about that person.

When people's work is valued, they will feel valued and make known where they would prefer to serve. This will help you identify future leaders and understand how they can best serve. Tim proved to be a leader in building and effectively using the gifts and interests of others. However, he told me his preference was to work independently. He was willing to work with others for the sake of the success of the gallery and to share the joy of it with others, but he preferred to work alone or with one or two others. Knowing this, I will strive to engage him in activities at church that honor his preference while including him in the mission of the church.

Building on the Best of the Past

The success of our art gallery did not occur in a vacuum. We already had a thriving fine arts ministry featuring the performing arts. One of the expressed dreams of that ministry was to expand it eventually to include the visual arts. So when the gallery came into its own, we were able to celebrate it as part of the history already established in our fine arts ministry.

It is effective to build current ministry movements on the past successes of the congregation. When we embarked upon our second capital drive, we reconstructed a history of St. Mark that celebrated the willingness of those from whom we have inherited this church to launch out, take risks, and extend in order to effectively serve not only those who were members at that time but others who might come. Established as a congregation in 1918, St. Mark took an enormous risk in 1953 to move to its present location. Following that decision, there were a series of building drives that saw the construction of two new worship centers in less than twenty years, the addition of a kitchen, and the conversion of a previous sanctuary into a fellowship hall. This missional past legitimized our future expansion as an extension of the historical character of St. Mark. This cherished history was both a celebration of our past as well as an inducement to reach out in mission in our time.

Connecting the present ministry to the past efforts of our congregations brings people together. The past is no longer used as a justification for not doing anything. Instead, it becomes the spur to faithful and fruitful action in the present. Building on the successes of the past acknowledges our responsibility to continue our ministry by looking at creative ways we can reach out in the name of Jesus Christ. Congregations that use the past to ward off the future will not have a future. Few of our churches were started with the goal of only surviving and serving the present. The vast majority of our churches were established and built with the vision of future generations worshiping and growing in faith within them. An effective strategy for moving into the future is to look for the best of the past and lift it up as a springboard for tomorrow. This is not always easy, and it rarely happens without mistakes.

* * *

I realized that I had not seen one couple at worship for a number of weeks. The following Sunday, I asked mutual friends about them.

They got quiet and finally said that the St. Mark they knew and loved no longer existed. There had been too many changes and too many new faces. They liked the old St. Mark with its small and intimate worship.

I was heartbroken. We had previously spent time together and discussed the growth of our church as the fulfillment of God's blessings to those who had held on for so long, praying for a rebirth of energy and joy. I hadn't realized until then that the growth of our congregation was not reenergizing for them; it was depersonalizing. I called and left a few messages, but they went unanswered. I prayed that eventually they would find a church home that would meet their needs.

No matter how leaders try to frame the opportunities and challenges before their churches, there will be those who will be uncomfortable with them. Some, like these friends, will leave. I am not sure what percentage of the congregation will leave as a result of growth and challenge. I have not seen any studies on it, but I think it is between 5 and 10 percent

We must change in the face of a changing world. The only question is how that change will occur. We can hang on and become a vestige of the hopes and dreams of those who established our churches—making them museums to the past—or we can dare to reach out and responsibly risk for the sake of mission. I am urging us to do just that.

There are contexts, however, where risking for mission and ministry is nearly impossible. If the church is located in a declining rural context or a deteriorating urban center, the opportunities for mission are limited. The choice is often between closing the church and moving or joining with another congregation. When the church my uncle and aunt had attended—where their children had been baptized, confirmed, and married—was no longer economically viable, they deeded the building to the county historical society. That church now stands as a monument to the past, and its faithful members have salted two or three other congregations.

Even when a congregation has the opportunity to move into mission and revitalized ministry, the sacrificial service and financial giving of the past ought to be celebrated as the foundation for God's future. One of the most effective processes in accomplishing this is to call a town hall meeting of the congregation for the sake of visioning. The agenda is simple: recall the best of our past and then ask what that would look like if we were to project it into our future. Set the ground rules for the exercise so that no idea, no matter how seemingly impossible or extravagant, is out of bounds. Allow for the creative, hopeful spirit of the past to imbue the group with ideas for the future. Then, when all the ideas are listed, ask the congregation to prioritize. I've given each person six little dots. Then I told them that they could put dots on the idea or ideas that they not only supported but would help fund. When the exercise is over, people are often surprised at what has surfaced as a top priority. Then, I take the priorities to the church council to begin the brainstorming on implementing the top three ideas. If you have more than three priorities you don't have priorities—you only have a list. When one of the three priorities has been accomplished, another makes the list. This can energize the congregation, refocus from the past and present to the future, and provide a road map forward.

The overall vision that directs this process ought to be a clear statement of the church's values, vision, and mission. Strive to engage the leadership first and then, thinking of concentric circles, more and more of the congregation in the process. In this way the congregation begins to own the future by helping to create it.

Permission-Giving Systems

Twenty-first-century leaders must create permission-giving systems that strive for coordination and alignment between emerging and existing ministries. Our church's first rummage sale started as an idea by two women in our congregation. One wanted to give back to the church by holding a sale but had no particular mission in mind. The other had a passion for making summer Bible camp participation possible for any and all of our children and young people regardless of their financial circumstances. These two women created a team, then met with our staff person whose job was to hold the new effort accountable to the pillars of our ministry and make certain that an appropriate process would ensure their success. With minimal disruption to ongoing ministries, the rummage sale proved highly successful.

Permission-giving systems open the congregation to new ideas from as many people as possible. These ideas are funneled through a process designed to say "yes" as often as possible. Committees are not required to validate the ideas. Neither the pastor nor lay leaders are required to approve of the ideas.

However, permission-giving systems don't mean that "anything goes." Instead, they strive to balance creativity, need-meeting ministries, and the critical culture elements that strengthen the identity of the church. The rummage sale endorsed the creativity of the team that emerged, clearly sought to meet the needs of families who would not or could not afford to send their children to summer camp, and embodied the values, vision, and mission of the congregation. If these three elements are not in balance, the idea will not work—and usually the participants themselves discover this. On occasion, it is the leader's job to communicate why a particular effort doesn't fit. Thankfully, that usually isn't necessary.

It has been said that the only thing more difficult than starting a new ministry in a congregation is letting go of one that is already dead. I have expended enormous energy trying to revitalize a ministry that at one time was vibrant and met needs. No matter how much time and energy I spent on those ministries, they almost always failed. Permission-giving systems acknowledge that any effort within the congregation that no longer creates interest and energy, engages member/disciples, and meets a clear set of needs will be terminated. Some of these ministries that have been terminated will resurface with a new vision and renewed purpose. Most, however, simply go away.

The difficulty is when some member/disciples remember the past fondly and expect the pastor or lay leader to single-handedly rejuvenate that ministry. The Christian leader needs to put the onus back on that member/disciple, giving him or her the clear expectation that any revitalization will be their responsibility. That usually ends the matter.

An example of this was our women's ministry. Based on the old model of "circles" in the church, it had simply run out of gas. The emergence of small groups, new women's Bible studies, and changing work patterns for many of the women of our congregation caused this ministry to struggle to stay alive. It still exists, though it is now smaller and more focused than it once was. In order for that to happen, staff and lay leaders had to accept that, no matter how many fond memories of its past we shared, the ministry as it then existed was dead. Those who cared about it could then decide to either let it die completely or refocus their energies with an activity that gave renewed purpose to a smaller and more effective form—which they did.

Permission-giving systems assume that new ideas can be embraced and established from anywhere in the congregation as long as they meet certain criteria. They must fit the culture of the church, and they must demonstrate viability by forming teams with clear leadership in place and find appropriate funding for themselves. But how do we determine if there is "culture fit"?

When I came to St. Mark, I found a congregation deeply committed to community service. At that time, we were also collecting AIDS kits for women in Tanzania. So I thought that we were ready for a global mission. I had a connection with a Lutheran pastor/evangelist in India. When he came to the United States to visit a daughter and her family, I invited him to St. Mark to speak, raise funds, and (I hoped) inspire member/disciples to engage in an international mission trip. There was a great deal of appreciation for his ministry and witness. The funds were raised. But there simply was not the requisite number of interested individuals to develop a mission engagement. Reflecting upon the opportunity he presented us, I discovered that the culture of St. Mark was shaped by a perception of limited resources that would be better used in the community. The value of community service was fully established, but there was no similar valuing of global outreach other than supporting denominational efforts.

Culture is the composite identity of a congregation. It is both the explicit and implicit values and attitudes of the people of the congregation. When a leader tests for cultural fit, she must be aware of both the stated elements of the congregational identity (values, vision, and mission) as well as the unstated aspects. These implicit elements are often more powerful than the explicit ones until they are brought into alignment. The unstated value at St. Mark was that our best missional efforts had been and would be in local community service. Collection of food for the local food pantry, gathering winter outer clothing for the homeless shelter, serving a meal at the mission downtown, and other such community service opportunities met with strong support and received significant response from the member/disciples of St. Mark. Global efforts were supported financially, but there was no cultural history or value for direct involvement. My efforts at an international mission trip failed because I didn't understand fully at that time the culture of St. Mark.

Since that time, as other international mission invitations have come, I have said no—not because they were not worthy, but because we are just now beginning to develop the culture that could embrace them. On the other hand, our community service options have multiplied, with greater involvement and support from our member/disciples. We can celebrate that cultural piece and, with a strategic and small first effort at global mission, help the congregation to grow a culture that will support both local and global mission.

When Christian leaders test for "culture fit," we begin to identify and clearly articulate the stated aspects of the culture. Then we review the successes and failures of the past to determine what unstated elements might be identified. If I had used that analysis, I would have been able to see that an immediate response to a global mission opportunity was probably not going to be possible. There had been no such involvement in the past at St. Mark. Also, there was no leader or team that was emerging to make it happen.

Testing for culture fit is important for two critical reasons. First, congregations, like individuals and families, are inundated with requests for support from worthy organizations and institutions. We need a solid reason to prioritize some and say no to others. Knowing the culture of the congregation helps us say no. Second, ministry efforts take time, energy, and resources. We ought to be wise stewards in marshaling these gifts for the best possible ministry initiatives. Knowing whether a potential ministry effort fits the culture will help the leader determine its likelihood for success.

Celebrating Success

Success in ministry and mission ought to be celebrated, and failures learned from. Too often we move quickly past the blessings God has given through a successful ministry effort. Instead, we ought to take the time to publicly thank God and those involved for what has happened. This is not to create an inappropriate pride. Instead, it creates an energy and joy that will lead to other efforts and invite more people into our ministries.

Just as we often move too quickly past our ministry success, we also want to bury our failures. In the church, this often takes the form of blaming an individual or our circumstances. The problem with blaming is that it frequently masks the real causes. When we assess blame, we ignore the systemic issues involved in blocking or defeating the ministry or mission endeavor. When I couldn't get the response required to launch a mission effort in India, I blamed myself. Only as time elapsed was I able to see the cultural realities involved. Individuals and even teams will not be successful in ministry or mission if learning from failure is not embraced as part of the congregational culture. It will always be viewed as separate from the "real" ministry of the congregation.

After every major effort at St. Mark, whether a perceived success or failure, we have a debriefing session. This is often at a staff meeting, with the assumption that the staff member most deeply involved will share our reflections afterward with the lay team involved so that they too can learn from their experience. When the rummage sale at St. Mark was over, the staff and lay team independently evaluated the experience. We learned that the timing was right; that it fit culturally because it was different from other significant fundraising activities; that clothing, assumed to be a significant part of the sales, was not purchased widely and much of it had to be given away;

and that having rooms for specific types of items was very helpful. The lay team also learned that selling large items on Craigslist or to individuals who saw them as they were collected was a positive element in the overall success of this venture.

The key for success in permission-giving ministry is continuous learning through constant evaluation. When permission-giving ministry is actively implemented, the learnings will not always be obvious. So, the leadership will need to assess the strengths and benefits of any ministry with courage and consistency. Once this process is in place, there is increased confidence throughout the system of ministry. Such confidence is possible when leaders accept and acknowledge their own imperfections in ministry so that perfection is no longer an unconscious expectation. As a consequence, ongoing evaluations are experienced as less judgmental and more opportunistic. Such assessments will rarely be resisted because they are not about guilt and blame but about learning and growing. This confidence will inspire new ministries and lead to the three mundane miracles addressed in the next chapter.

6

Three Keys to Effective Ministry

Leadership is, admittedly, hard work. That work can be sustained as leaders focus on building and sustaining three things: enthusiasm, focus, and momentum. These are first sequential, and subsequently circular. Enthusiasm is the energy to make useful change and build on the best of the past. Focus directs that energy so that it can be maximized to accomplish so much more than the scattered energy of various efforts can. Momentum is the result of these two at work within a congregation. Momentum will, in turn, feed the enthusiasm and reinforce the focus of the ministry. I hope this chapter will inspire leaders to evaluate how these three keys are functioning in the congregation and take action to implement them.

Enthusiasm

Enthusiasm in the local church is not a momentary burst of energy. Rather, it is the sustained spiritual energy of a congregation focused on its mission and vision for ministry. The people of God know that we are called into mission. Mission is not just something we do, nor is it a particular committee or team within the congregation. Mission is fundamental to who we are. Without a clear commitment to mission that is stated, celebrated, and lifted up continuously by leaders, congregations suffer spiritual depression. This ennui is evident when all the members' efforts are spent on trying to maintain or prop up the current activities or past legacies of the church. This is a congregation that is merely surviving, not thriving. Thriving congregations are challenged congregations.

I never would have chosen to lead St. Mark into a capital drive in my first year of ministry there. However, the opportunity arose to purchase of a building contiguous to our property. Through the excellent work of a lay team, an appropriate price was negotiated and, with the approval of 89 percent of the congregation, we made the purchase. The result was an outpouring of energy that even outstripped the financial support.

Enthusiasm exploded within the congregation. We were a church on the move! This really began before I arrived. The congregation had already remodeled the sanctuary into a lovely worship space. Then they looked for a pastor committed to growing the church. There are many fine pastors that could have met that criterion, but they ended up calling me. I entered a congregation that was already eager to move ahead. Before I came, I read the results of a study the church had conducted and discovered that 71 percent wanted to reach out to the unchurched. This was clear evidence of a growing spiritual desire to be in mission.

Enthusiasm is the spiritual outcome of reaching out, trying new things, and, with a willingness to risk and the responsible consideration of costs, deciding to do something. If any of these attributes are short-circuited in the congregation, enthusiasm will not emerge. When it does emerge, there is a burst of energy, giving, and joy that is palpable even in personal conversations, and also in the worship attendance and giving of the whole church.

If a pastor or Christian leader desires to create enthusiasm, he will gauge the present commitments and hopes of the congregation.

Then, identifying an opportunity that embodies these, he will challenge the church to pray about it, talk to one another about it, and then act. This process builds upon the present but demands extending in mission. The buzz created begins building enthusiasm in the church. That buzz—if managed positively—will lead to appropriate action. The action will be the affirmation of the church's need to be a people in mission. The people know that the Great Commission is at the heart of being Christ's church. The leader's responsibility is to find the needs and opportunities that will challenge the people of God to risk becoming who we know we are called to be. When the first successful project is followed by a second, and then a third, we will have created a culture of expectation. The people of God will anticipate the next challenge. This translates into a continuous expectation of ministry, sustained and expanded to meet newly identified needs.

The task of the leader, when enthusiasm and the expectation of growing ministry come together, is to channel the resulting energy back into the congregation so that creativity can grow into new ministries. The leader channels these efforts by constantly lifting up the values, vision, and mission of the church and connecting the energy to their expression. As we celebrate new ministries, we articulate how they help us fulfill our mission and lead us toward achieving our vision.

When our director of youth and young adults wanted to give teen Bibles to our first-year confirmation students, I wasn't sure that was a ministry that fit. At St. Mark, we hold a ceremony during worship where parents present their children with a Bible when they are in the third grade. This embodies our commitment to support and encourage the fulfillment of baptismal promises in the families of our congregation. So I asked her to justify this expense. She reminded me that we are committed to "making disciples across generations with real faith for real life" (our vision statement), and that if we were serious about achieving that vision we would need to equip our young people with Scriptures that they could easily access and understand. The goal was to help them "grow in faith, share Jesus Christ, and serve others" by giving them a Bible that fit their time of life. As a result, on the Sunday that we give third graders Bibles, we have also set aside a service to share a "teen Bible" with our first-year confirmation students. They use these Bibles in our confirmation program and are encouraged to read them at home. She was channeling the energy and resources of our ministry of confirmation to help us achieve our mission and move toward our vision.

Focus

If someone asked a member/disciple of your congregation what their church was about, could they answer? At St. Mark, I believe the vast majority of our member/disciples would say, "Discipleship." This is the result of reiterating the vision over and over again. This is the result of using discipleship language throughout our ministry: in sermons, publicity, and messaging. One of our buildings is called the Discipleship Center, and the other the Worship Center. They embody the focus of our ministry: worship and discipleship.

I had a conversation with a member at St. Mark who is a sixty-something, old-line Lutheran. I wasn't sure how she would respond to the new format of the Wednesday teaching service. But she had come faithfully, and now I knew why. She said, "I've loved these Wednesday evening teaching worship events. I've grown so much in my faith that I know I am a better disciple for it. And isn't that the point?"

"Yes, that is the point," I replied. "We want to use whatever format or method we can to equip you . . ."

"I know, I know," she interrupted. "With a real faith for real life."

Driving home, I said a prayer of thanksgiving to God. This old-line member of our congregation was becoming a disciple. She knew that faith for the Christian in the twenty-first century is not something that can be left on its own but needs to be nurtured. It demands expression in the everyday life of the believer. Her sharing told me that our teaching service was on target.

The decision to launch a Wednesday evening teaching service was born of practical considerations. We were leading the congregation through *The Story* Bible, and we wanted to get through its thirty-one chapters in the weeks available to us. The solution was to preach in the weekend services on one aspect of *The Story* and then expand on it Wednesday evenings. But practical considerations were not the only factor. New programming at St. Mark has to have a clear discipleship focus. So while I'd be able, in the forty-five to fifty minutes of teaching, to go into greater historical and theological detail, I would have to shape the sessions to lead to questions and applications for the life of each disciple who attended. Each session would need to include a challenge to apply the lessons or truths shared.

Focus makes enthusiasm possible. Enthusiasm is nothing more than energy with a clear focus. At St. Mark, the focus is always on equipping our member/disciples with a more active faith life. Discipleship is the invitation to grow in our ability to reflect our faith in our everyday lives. We do not do this perfectly and never will. But the encouragement is always to apply our faith to another area of our lives.

* * *

When the car cut me off on the major freeway through Des Moines,

I was immediately angry. After all, that driver was supposed to yield to traffic on the freeway as she entered from the ramp. As my blood pressure increased, I thought, "What's she doing in my lane?!"

When I shared that story on Wednesday night, the crowd laughed. I knew it wasn't just at me: they were identifying with me! Most of them had thought something similar or been angry in the same way over the same kind of intrusion—as if the freeway, or at least our particular lane, belonged to us! Then I asked the question that had occurred to me on the freeway that day: What if she is facing an emergency and needs to get somewhere as quickly as possible? If that were the case and we knew it, I asked, wouldn't that change our response? And if we are to love others as we are loved and forgive others as we have been forgiven, shouldn't we put the best possible construction on the behavior of that driver? Shouldn't we pray that if she needed to get somewhere fast, she would do so and arrive there safely?

Focus on a more active faith life is the constant theme that runs through our messages and ministries. Without it, congregations meander with disparate efforts and distracted leaders.

Disciple-making ministries are focused on a single desired outcome: a living faith. Such a faith is founded in the word of God, nurtured in the church, and expressed, however imperfectly, in our daily life. Spiritual disciplines are lifted up and practiced not as ends in themselves but because they grow us toward that outcome. Daily prayer and Bible reading, weekly worship, serving others, small groups, and tithing are all practices of faith that help us cross the intangible—and some would argue unreal—line that exists between worship and the world. This is our focus. This is the goal of all of our ministry and efforts. In the multi-tasking of ministry, this is the North Star to which we return again and again to make certain that we are still on course.

In order to foster living faith, the disciple-leader needs a radical trust in the power of the Holy Spirit in two significant aspects of the life of discipleship. The first is the spiritual growth of the disciples. For far too long pastors have taken responsibility for the spiritual health and growth of the member/disciples of our congregations. The truth is that people's spiritual well-being is between them and God. The role of the pastor or Christian leader is to provide the raw materials for faith formation, the challenge to put faith to the test, and the opportunities for such growth within the life of the congregation. This trust in the work of the Holy Spirit is also an active respect for the right of the individual to make decisions before God. We cannot make decisions for others. We can articulate the consequences of wrong decisions and pray for our people—placing them in the care of the God we know in Jesus Christ.

Fostering living faith also takes an audacious trust in the Holy Spirit in a second aspect of the Christian life: our willingness to witness to Jesus Christ. I believe evangelism is an outcome of discipleship. My experience leads me to conclude that evangelism is not a program in the church but an extension of its life of faith. When people grow deep in their relationship with Jesus Christ, they cannot help but share it with others. On the other hand, I think that without such a living relationship, evangelism is tacked on to the mission of the congregation without any passion or real commitment to it. In fact, the data is clear: with all the evangelism committees in all of the Protestant churches in the United States, worship attendance and overall giving is still in decline. What we need is a rebirth of following Jesus, which will lead to sharing his love in word and deed.

We live in a time of pluralism and spiritual relativism. Disciples of Jesus will witness for the sake of the hope and joy we uniquely have as Christians. It's not about who is going to heaven and who is going to hell. Only God has the invitation list. It's about being the church and not being a club. Clubs exist only for the sake of their members, and membership growth is for the sake of the club. But the Christian church was established for the sake of the world. We live beyond ourselves when we dare to witness to Jesus as a peculiar manifestation of God both in history and in our lives today. Unless we truly believe that there is a unique spiritual gift that comes through Jesus Christ, we will have little to say to our world. How we understand that uniqueness will shape our witness.

The question is not, "How can we grow the church?" The real question is, "How can we call others to faith and equip them for a living faith?" When pastors keep the focus on the personal growth and experience of others with Jesus Christ, the Holy Spirit will raise up people to live the gospel in word and deed. That is ultimately God's work, not ours. We do the best we can so that the Holy Spirit might be at work in and through us, keeping our eyes focused on the goal of discipleship.

Momentum

When congregational enthusiasm is aligned with focus, the result is the third key for fruitful church life: momentum. Momentum is the collective surge of energy and creativity that builds from the enthusiasm and focus of the member/disciples of a congregation. It is palpable as more and more people become engaged in fruitful ministry and mission as part of the ministry of discipleship.

Growing and maintaining momentum requires adding to enthusiasm and focus a system for volunteer recognition, engagement, and support. For this system to be put in place, pastors must develop habits of affirmation as well as practices of recognition. There are many habits of affirmation than can be put into practice. Let me suggest two: the habit of thanking volunteers, and thank you cards.

"Thank you," I said as Nila bustled into the sanctuary to set up for our worship service on a typical Saturday afternoon. The ladder was in place for changing the "eternal light," the paraments for the new season were being brought out, and another member of our altar guild was in the sacristy preparing the elements for Holy Communion. When I thanked her, she just smiled. I don't want her to think that I take for granted the work she and the other members of her team do. Later, I entered the sacristy to thank the two working there as well. There was a time when I would have simply said hello and walked on. But I have learned that appropriate informal recognition goes a long way in affirming the value of service. Since then, I have tried to practice the habit of a simple "thank you" as I pass. I call it a "drive-by affirmation."

Another habit that I learned from a colleague was cards of thanks. I try to write five thank you cards each week to volunteers whose service I appreciate. I keep a list of those I've thanked, since I don't want to send two cards in three weeks. My handwriting is awful, but the response to these handwritten notes has been deep appreciation. These are brief notes—never more than a sentence or two—that genuinely express my appreciation for the willingness and follow-through of the individual in a specific service to the congregation or to me. Typed or e-mail notes of gratitude have never led to the expressions of gratitude I receive for these barely legible scribblings.

Public recognition can be helpful as well. Each year at St. Mark we identify three to five key volunteers whose service has gone far beyond the norm. These people are publicly identified and certificates are given that identify them as a "Volunteer of the Year." We have never experienced a negative backlash from this practice, as many believed we would. Instead, we have had member/disciples identify others who might be recognized and why. These public displays of gratitude also allow us to lift up the critical element of service to the church for everyone and thank those who share their gifts and talents for the sake of our ministry.

A system that recognizes and thanks volunteers must also be a system that habitually supports them. One of the ways we do that at St. Mark is our "twenty-four-hour rule." We have established an expectation that a staff member will respond to a phone call or e-mail from one of our member/disciples within twenty-four hours. Even if an answer to their concern cannot be given, we can close the communication loop and let them know we have received their question and cannot respond but will get back to them as soon as possible. This tells the volunteer that we have both received their communication and will process it. We do not always do this perfectly, and there may be times when an immediate response is not necessary. But this needs to be an intentional decision, not just setting it aside.

All of these strategies keep the momentum going. Jim Collins, in his book *Built to Last,* speaks of this as a flywheel. It takes effort to get the flywheel moving but, once it is moving, it takes less and less effort to keep it going. That's been my experience with momentum and the strategies to keep it building in the congregation.

Any of these strategies will be enhanced by continually sharing the focus of our overall ministry as well as the matter at hand. People want to know that their efforts are valued and that they are part of something bigger than themselves. The effective Christian leader looks for ways to connect the disparate efforts of many volunteers to the values, vision, and mission of the congregation as it applies to their specific engagement. Reiterating our key messages is critical in implementing and working the three keys for fruitful congregational life. Just about the time a leader thinks she has communicated the key messages so often that it is no longer necessary, member/disciples are just starting to both understand and identify them.

* * *

"I think I'm beginning to get this stuff about relating to others for spiritual growth," he said.

"Oh, have you joined a small group?" I asked.

"No," he replied, looking like he'd just sucked on a lemon. "What I mean is that, since I've started this discipleship business I've found I can't treat my employees the way I used to. I've always tried to treat them with respect," he hastened to add, "but I didn't want to get mixed up in their lives or take time to hear what's happening with them outside of the plant. But now I can't do that any longer. This 'relating to others for spiritual growth' means I see them in a very different way." Seeing my smile, he said, "Now, I'm not perfect, Pastor Mike. But I am changing. And, you know what, I kind of like it; I just thought you'd like to know."

When the focuses of our ministry have become clear to our member/disciples, they begin to practice them in their lives. When that happens, the Holy Spirit will lead them into new ways of seeing and acting beyond what the leader originally imagined. It had never occurred to me until that conversation that "relating to others for spiritual growth" could mean anything other than joining a small group. That businessman's vision expanded my understanding and appreciation for what the Holy Spirit can do with enthusiasm, focus, and momentum. I couldn't help but think of our Lord's teaching about faith as a mustard seed—plant it, tend it, and then watch God grow it!

7

Culture Change: The Value of Persistence

Congregations can be noisy organizations. The noise can come from unavoidable conflict and disagreement, which is experienced as resistance. Resistance is an unavoidable by-product of leadership. If pastors and leaders understand it this way, they will be better equipped to both handle and address it.

Besides resistance, there is another source of noise in the congregation: lack of clear values. Every institution has core values. These values may not be clearly stated, but they are implemented in making the significant decisions and in the common interactions of the member/disciples of each church. Identifying the core values at work within a congregation will help explain behaviors and attitudes present in that church as well as create an opportunity to implement new values that better reflect the vision and mission of that congregation.

This chapter will address these two sources of noise, and will conclude with a discussion of accountability systems that can promote health and vitality in ministry.

Facing Resistance

"No thank you," he said tersely. I had greeted him at the door to our worship center and asked if he'd be willing to help us in our capital drive. His response caught me by surprise. I had known him and his wife since first coming to St. Mark. We had shared activities and, I thought, got along well. I simply said "OK" and left it at that. In two weeks, they were visiting other congregations, and within a month had left St. Mark.

I am always sad whenever an individual or a family chooses to leave the congregation I am serving, but it is often inevitable. Christian leaders who are committed to growing the church will meet resistance. This resistance will take many forms. Sometimes it will be a quiet undercurrent of displeasure with a particular decision. At other times there will be friction in the congregation. The couple I mentioned above handled their disagreement with the decision of the congregation—by an overwhelming majority—in a responsible manner. They chose to leave rather than cause disruption in the church. Those who disagree with the decisions of the leadership have a right to do so. However, they do not have the right to derail the decisions of the leadership and congregation. The problem is that, unless those who disagree can eventually align with the decisions, their disapproval will frequently "leak." By that I mean that it takes a mature disciple to disagree with decisions, choose to stay in the church, and keep the emotions and opinions of their disagreements to themselves. More often, the feelings and opinions will color how even well-intentioned individuals see and experience the shared life of the congregation.

There are often ways to work through disagreements. Leaders can, for example, meet with people and try to talk through the resistance. This can be effective if those involved can respectfully agree to disagree. When there is no respect for a differing opinion, the disagreement will continue beneath the surface and influence how those involved experience and judge the ongoing life of the church.

Resistance from Conflicting Vision

A conflict of vision, for example, can only be resolved in the above process. The congregation can only go in one direction at a time. The best that can be hoped for in a conflict of vision is for one vision to be pursued while the other is on hold to become an alternative in the future. But vision, as we have discussed above, creates an energy and momentum that often makes an alternative impossible as time goes on. Nonetheless, in matters like building programs or other physical or ministry options, a compromise may be possible.

"Pastor Mike, when will we call an associate pastor?" he asked. This leader at St. Mark was asking a question I had heard a number of times. Having only recently assumed the senior pastor role, I responded, "Now is not the time. I haven't been here long enough for us to have set the vision or established the style into which I would invite another pastor." Then I continued, "I want you to know that I hear you—and others have asked the same question. I am convinced that we will eventually call another pastor. It's just that right now, I don't think it would be wise. We need to work together for a while."

My friend was satisfied with that response, and we are planning for the calling of another pastor in the future. In the short term, the leadership endorsed the growth of our staff through lay ministry and staff. This has helped us grow our ministry, our leadership, and our financial base. When our vision leads us to a second full-time pastor, we will begin our search. This was a case where it was acceptable to wait for a secondary vision to be implemented after the primary vision was in place. The achieving of one vision may only mean postponing another.

Resistance from Conflicting Values

Resistance can also be created by the congregation's core values. These values determine what is acceptable, and every congregation has them, whether they are stated or implicit. Any significant change in the life or direction of the congregation can challenge these core values.

At St. Mark, a vision for survival emerged after a protracted season of conflict. This vision unconsciously led to tolerance as an implicit core value. By the time I had been called to serve as senior pastor, the congregation had already moved past a vision of survival. Through the good work of my predecessor and the lay leadership, St. Mark was beginning to grow and look toward the future. Tolerance, however, was still shaping our congregational life in unhelpful ways. One of the signs of this was the use of well-worn card tables for sign-up sheets and the collection of goods for those in need in the gathering space. With tolerance as a core value, the appearance of the tables and the heaps of goods for those in need was not a problem. The habit of tolerating clutter had been established. And because it was the way things had always been done, the potential impact on visitors as well as on the image of the congregation was not understood nor addressed. More than these cosmetic issues, tolerance encouraged—not just allowed—individuals to work outside of their gifts and passions, with predictable results.

With the congregation's transition from a vision for survival into a new vision for a thriving ministry, there was added a pastoral change. This change in leadership brought new eyes to evaluate decisions. This evaluation led to a growing commitment to cleaning the culture as part of raising the confidence and self-identity of the congregation. The core value of tolerance was no longer effectively reflecting the commitments of the member/disciples at St. Mark, nor was it helping to move the church forward. As this evaluative process emerged over time, the value of tolerance was identified and replaced. The resistance to this change of values was experienced first in those who had spent time working from it and reinforcing it. One of the most visible signs of this conflict occurred when a ministry leader was replaced because he was working outside of his gift set. That misplacement, and the value of tolerance that had given rise to it, had caused a very visible ministry to miss the mark.

Tolerance is not the same as grace. Grace is the response to the reality of sin. Grace takes seriously behaviors and outcomes that need care. Tolerance suggests that such care is unnecessary. In the case of the misplaced leader, his friends were angry that he was no longer in that leadership role. The leadership of the congregation understood and supported the new value of excellence and stood with me as I dealt with the situation. What most of his friends didn't know was his sense of relief at being removed from a position for which he was not gifted by skills or temperament. Later, he was invited into a different leadership role, and that ministry has multiplied three times over.

The value of tolerance leads to a culture of codependence. The assumption is that the role of the church and its leadership—especially the pastor—is to make everyone happy. That is impossible. Moving from tolerance as a core value to excellence at St. Mark provided the opportunity to lift up our values, vision, and mission, and articulate how decisions were being made that aligned with them.

Resistance that comes from a values conflict is often disguised as something else. In our case, the moving of the card tables and collection of goods for the poor were perceived as "putting on airs." The change of leadership was done with appropriate process and was perceived as an issue of "the control of the pastor." Knowing the values and outcomes toward which the congregation is working and clearly articulating them to leaders, staff, and the congregation will help the pastor navigate the accusations that always come with resistance. In conversation with other leaders and staff, the pastor or Christian leader will also have the opportunity to have her convictions and perceptions tested. Sometimes, the leader's understanding of the issues is not accurate. Discovering this early on is very helpful because once resistance turns into conflict—which can happen very quickly—positions tend to solidify and be polarized. In the twenty-first-century church, we want resistance and conflict to be managed as close to the events as possible. And we want to be assured that our perceptions are real!

Strategies for Dealing with Resistance

Resistance tends to be covert and to attempt to "delegate up"—that is, it will want to make an appeal to the highest level of authority. There are two strategies that can be helpful to the leader in dealing with these characteristics of resistance.

First, name it. Without any name-calling of individuals, name the core problem. In our case, I named it "clutter." I shared with the congregation in meetings and sermons that I would never invite guests into my house without first cleaning it up. If I didn't clean and straighten my house before my guest arrived, it would communicate my lack of value for my friends and my self-identity. Most of us know that a messy home is a reflection on the homeowner. Did we really want others to come into St. Mark and make judgments on our ministry based upon clutter? Over time, the congregation has fully endorsed this expression of the value of excellence.

Second, prevent resistance's tendency to delegate up by handling legitimate concerns as close to the person and circumstances as possible. The issues of clutter and misplaced leadership have never come to our church council. We want to deal with honest disagreements and conflicts at the lowest level in the church possible. Only when it is of such a serious nature and involves many people will resistance come before the church council. Democracy doesn't mean that each incidence of resistance must get a public hearing before leaders.

Resistance is a natural part of change. Christian leaders need to anticipate it and then develop practices to appropriately deal with it. Resistance, when rightly viewed, can teach us things we would probably not learn any other way.

Creating the Vision and Mission

The questions of how to find a vision or develop a mission statement are good ones—but they are the wrong ones. The questions that begin to open the door to vision and mission are, first, What do you want your church to accomplish over the next five to ten years? That question will help you begin to articulate your vision. The second question is, How will you get there?

To answer the first question, imagine your church accomplishing a great task for the kingdom of God. What would that be? Is this vision compelling enough to engage enough people with enough energy for a long enough time to lead to the future—particularly God's future for that ministry? The initial answer to this question always comes from a leader. I have never seen a compelling or effective vision emerge from a group of people. At St. Mark, our vision—*making disciples across generations with real faith for real life*—was developed as I shared my vision for St. Mark to be a disciple-making church. Then we began to answer the second question when a small group focused on *real faith for real life.* We added and adopted the cross-generational aspect in a town-hall conversation. The vision makes it clear that we are about making disciples. It also asserts that we will purposefully reach out and engage people across generational lines. Notice that it does not have a denominational reference. We want to be a congregation that welcomes and equips people for a living faith that isn't separate from their everyday lives; it doesn't matter to us if they are Lutheran in background or not.

This doesn't mean that we are embarrassed about being Lutheran. In fact, if you look at what we teach and preach, how we approach worship and our organization, you'll see that we are intentionally *Lutheran*. But we follow Luther's own view: in response to hearing that those who agreed with his positions were being called *Lutherans*, he said, "What is Luther if not rubbish? It is enough to be called Christian." Our goal is to lift up Jesus Christ.

The mission is the strategy adopted and expressed by your congregation that will reflect who you are as a church and help you best move toward accomplishing your vision. At St. Mark, our mission—*Grow in Faith, Share Jesus Christ, and Serve Others*—was adopted before I arrived. The congregation had begun a process during the ministry of my predecessor that led to its adoption. An interim pastor used it frequently enough that many in the congregation knew it by heart. I liked that it had action words, was short, and, if implemented, would certainly help us achieve our vision. So we kept it.

Christian leaders catch sight of a vision when they can identify and articulate the ultimate purpose of their ministry. Over the past twenty years, effective ministries have become more and more *outcome-based*. This means that simply replicating what has been is no longer effective. Maintaining a particular tradition may be a significant element in the ministry of a church (and often is!), but it is no longer compelling for the vast majority of people. People are willing to give more energy, time, and financial resources to a compelling vision.

With a clear vision, the people know where they are going, why they are here, and can celebrate whenever and wherever they see it happening.

Every ministry ought to have a vision statement and then develop a mission statement that identifies actions that will move the church to accomplishing its mission. The mission statement should be made of action words and be short. If there is a narrative mission statement, it ought to be abbreviated to a short phrase with three key elements. This fits the idea that priorities limit our options to three at a time.

Whereas vision statements arise from the vision of a leader and then are expanded by the congregation, the mission statement can be developed out of focused congregational conversation. Leaders will need to facilitate that conversation and, often, develop the abbreviated form. But sometimes that comes from the congregation itself.

Core Values

As discussed above, every organization has core values that are often unconscious. Pastors need to work with an eye to identifying the values that determine what is acceptable in the ministry of that church. A good way to start is by developing a list of possible values to test with the key events or ministries of the congregation. Once a short list of core values has been identified, the leader should test the accuracy of his observations with other leaders and trusted members of the church. The next step is to engage the key leadership in identifying the values that will shape the future of the congregation. Some may already be functioning, while others may need to be developed.

Our leadership team met on a day-long retreat. One of the tasks was to clarify our core values—those values that would ground our work and to which our ministries would be held accountable. After a brainstorming session in which over thirty values had been named, we began to eliminate those that were not acceptable or would not empower us to lead our congregation into the future. After a lengthy conversation that reflected on the past, present, and vision for the future of our ministry, we identified four core values: discipleship, integrity, community, and excellence. Of the four, three were already shaping the culture and life of St. Mark to one degree or another. The fourth, excellence, was not. That didn't mean that there weren't excellent ministries or efforts, but overall the ministry did not expect excellence. We also agreed that all four needed to be articulated and shared with the congregation so that we could develop attitudes, behaviors, and systems that would be built from and accountable to these four core values.

How many core values can a church have? I don't have any research on it, but I don't think you'll have more than three to five core values that really function. You want your core values to be so strong that they provide an automatic evaluation process for your ministries.

Once core values are identified and shared by the leadership, they need to be put to use. At St. Mark, if it doesn't have to do with discipleship, we don't do it. If it can't be done in a manner that strengthens our community and with integrity, we won't do it. And if we can't find a way to do it with excellence, it will be dropped. These core values continue to shape our ministry and are increasingly unconscious in the life of our church. I am confident that they will stay effective for a long time. In fact, we have had visitors who can identify how these values are experienced.

As a word of warning, violation of core values must have consequences. One such violation led to the eventual dismissal of a staff member. That was a painful experience, as you might imagine. But the violation of our core values was obvious, and our very identity was on the line. Don't identify your core values unless you want them to have teeth. Unconscious core values already have teeth; that's why you can identify them by observing what is actually going on in your church.

Rewriting our Beliefs

"What's wrong with the Apostles' Creed?" he asked. "It seems to have stood the test of time and I don't think we can do any better. Why do we need a St. Mark belief statement?"

He had a good point. We use the Apostles' Creed at most of our worship services. I replied, "I don't think we can improve on the Apostles' Creed. The problem is that most people don't understand it. So we'd like to share our orthodox beliefs in a statement that anyone can understand."

He thought for a moment, and then grudgingly said, "You've got a point there, Pastor Mike. As long as we don't get rid of the Apostles' Creed but use this one to help people, I guess it's OK."

There was a time when anyone could visit any Lutheran church—or congregation of any denomination—of a particular variety and experience the same worship, the same creed, and even sing the same hymns. That was a time when the language of the Judeo-Christian heritage was also a part of our culture. We also had denominational loyalty, so that Lutherans or Methodists tended to only visit churches with those identifications. None of these factors are real in the twenty-first century. As a consequence, many of those who visit may or may not be able to identify what a particular congregation actually believes.

People who worship want to be able to understand what a particular congregation holds to be true in both doctrine and practice. In fact, over the past twenty or thirty years, we have seen people repeatedly visit for months before deciding to become part of a church. They are often testing to see what is being taught about the Bible and other aspects of the life of faith. Only when they are comfortable in their ability to know that will they take the step to join a congregation. Stating clearly and in contemporary language what we believe helps them in that process. If the beliefs and core values of a congregation are clear and consistently upheld, people will become comfortable and will identify with the church. If they are not, many will never take that step or will do so only to lapse into inactivity as they learn more about the congregation. Neither of these are discipleship outcomes. People who are serious enough about their faith journey to visit a new congregation, with all the anxiety that often entails, will also want to know what that church stands for.

Accountability Systems

"I hate this," she said. "Am I expecting too much?"

I was discussing a new hire with a key member of our team at St. Mark. We make it clear that, as a disciple-making church, there are no jobs—only calls to serve God by serving the church in a specific role. The adjustment of the new hire had been a difficult one, since she had moved from a corporate setting to the ministry of our congregation. Now, three months into the work, this staff member was struggling with her performance.

"No, I don't think you expect too much," I replied. "I think the question really is whether there has been enough time for her to make the transition. I know you have been clear about your expectations. I heard you articulate them and they are in the job description. Is it time to let her sink or swim?"

"I have to get back to my real job. I think next week I'll let her know that I can't provide the daily instruction or backup I've given. That way we can see where she is."

Three weeks later, I found out that the assessment of our new hire had moved in a very different direction. She had made the adjustments necessary and was fast becoming someone on whom we could rely.

Accountability systems are in place so that the quality of our ministries can be evaluated and those responsible for them can know how they are doing. Ministry can be a good place to hide. It can also be a very confusing area of work because so much of what we do is "soft"—that is, it defies clear measurements. In order for systems to be effective, they must be implemented at the top. Accountability systems begin with the leadership, the pastor.

Accountability is not the same thing as control, however. I would like to suggest an "accountability continuum." On the left is control. On the right is not accountability, but abdication. The majority of our congregations function out of abdication. That is to say, we tend to let people, volunteers and staff, function with minimal supervision and sketchy job descriptions. The problem with this is that we don't clearly articulate our expectations. As a consequence, our people do not know when they have succeeded or failed.

Accountability is at the center of the continuum. This allows the person in charge to move either left, exercising greater control, or right, granting more freedom for the individual to act independently depending upon their performance. When we too quickly abdicate supervision, we often leave the person without the support needed to succeed. When we function from the control side of the continuum, we manage the details as well as the person. Accountability connects the individual to a clearly defined task that fits within the values, vision, and mission of the church.

Formal accountability systems usually take time to implement and are slow to deal with problems. The best accountability systems are operational on a daily basis. They become habits for success. At St.

Mark, I meet with the president of the church council one-on-one at least once a month—before our Executive Committee meeting. We discuss not only what is on the agenda for that meeting but other issues in the church. This is a respectful but "no-holds-barred" conversation. I learn of issues and concerns that I am not always aware of. I also have a chance to test ideas, hopes, and dreams with him or her.

The Executive Committee has five members and meets once a month. This is my second accountability team. Because of the sensitive nature of personnel issues and pastoral concerns, this is the small group to whom I report and seek guidance. When I have a difficult decision to make, the president and Executive Committee are the first to hear of it and comment on it.

I also am accountable to the entire church council of ten, but this accountability is more general in nature. These are the caretakers of the mission and vision of St. Mark. Major planning and fiduciary responsibilities begin with them. Their resolutions and direction are critical in the operations of our congregation. I do not have 1400 bosses. I have one, then five, and then ten.

I also believe that accountability moves in both directions, so I encourage my staff to give me appropriate feedback and criticism. I make it clear that I do not take such feedback well in public, but I rely on it. One of my maxims is, "It's not what I know that can hurt me; it's what I don't know that can hurt me." The staff and leadership of the congregation help me know what I need to know.

Leaders in the twenty-first-century church cannot afford to be isolated from the member/disciples in ministry in the church. I go out of my way to learn as many names of our member/disciples as possible and use those names as frequently as possible. I have learned that this opens the door for open communication and demonstrates my desire to affirm the value of our people. Accessibility is a key to accountability systems.

* * *

"I am so grateful for your willingness to take the time and make our worship space so beautiful," I said.

She and her husband had spent hours decorating our worship space for Christmas. The gossamer swags, white lights, and stars illuminated our worship space in a wonderful way.

"You are welcome," she said with a smile. "We just love how it looks and couldn't bear to see it decorated in any other way."

I am not a project manager. But since our volunteer to oversee the Advent-Christmas decorating of the worship center had taken a job and couldn't be present to shepherd the process of decorating for the holidays, I was the one in charge. Small groups had been recruited for the task, with each assigned a specific part of the decorating so that no one would be overburdened. They arrived to help early, and each began the work guided by pictures from the previous year as well as our collective memory. The result was beautiful. Accountability would be immediate: those who came would see their work. The feedback was strong and positive. We had done our job. The response to the decorations in both our worship center and discipleship center was marvelous.

Accountability systems require a person to monitor the outcomes of ministry. In the case above, the congregation would be the final arbiter of our success, but any leader could become the one responsible. That means that when it doesn't work, an identifiable leader is responsible to evaluate and articulate what happened and why for any given project. This creates a system of accountability that is part of the fabric of ministry. Any of us involved in the ministry assume that we are accountable for the result—the success or failure as judged by the desired outcomes of the ministry—of any activity within St. Mark. The consequence is an ongoing evaluative process.

* * *

"Pastor Mike, I'm sorry for what happened," he said. The PowerPoint of our worship service had been interrupted by a technical glitch. "Oh," I said, "That's OK. I know that you did the best you could."

"Well," he replied, "that may be true, but I'm sorry that we couldn't get it right. I just want it to work the way it's supposed to work."

"Thank you, Rick," I said. "I am so grateful for your willingness to make it work."

At St. Mark, we are all in the work of making it right together. Rick is a part-time audio-visual technician. His concern for the presentation of our worship experience is symptomatic of our accountability systems at work. We do not expect perfection. We do expect excellence. Rick knows this, and as a devout Roman Catholic he has signed on to make our worship experience the best possible encounter with God through Scripture, prayer, and preaching. This self-evaluative process tells the leader when the accountability systems are in place. Once the leader has adopted this approach to leading the ministry of the congregation, it will permeate the church. I was so relieved with Rick's self-evaluation. It reinforced the truth that our systems were in place and working.

Conclusion

I have attempted in this book to speak as a pastor to pastors and other congregational leaders because I am convinced the Christian church in our time needs equipped leaders. I hope my convictions and opinions create reflection and conversation among pastors and leaders so that faithful and fruitful ministry is the result. I recognize that all leadership is contextual, so the application of the ideas in this book will vary from one setting to another. But the general thrust has been to engage Christian leaders in conversation and reflection on ministry at a strategic level. I also hope that this book will help to dismiss the predicted demise of the congregation. This doesn't mean that the shape of our churches will not change. But the primary expression of the communion of saints is the local congregation, and I am convinced that we can anticipate a rebirth of vitality and mission no matter what form the congregation eventually takes. My basic conviction is that disciple-making ministry is the model for the twenty-first-century church. The church is outfitted by the Holy Spirit for this work and this time.

Ministry is hard work. Ministry is also incredibly rewarding work. Christian leaders are privileged to catch a glimpse of the work of the Holy Spirit to bring healing and transformation to the lives of those we serve. We celebrate the spiritual life through Baptism and the Lord's Supper; we mark the continuing saga of humanity in marriage; and we are privileged to sit with the dying and witness the transition from mortality to immortality. No other organization on earth has this range of encounters with God and humankind.

I hope you will join me in prayerful celebration of our commission and the privilege and promise of this work we call ministry! May our God bless us as we seek to faithfully and fruitfully continue the ministry of Christ's church. My prayer is this: let your kingdom grow, O God, in your churches. Amen.

List of Works Cited

Collins, Jim, and Jerry I. Porras. *Built to Last: Successful Habits of Visionary Companies*. New York: HarperBusiness, 2004.

Foss, Michael W. *Power Surge: Six Marks of Discipleship for a Changing Church*. Minneapolis: Fortress Press, 2009.

Ebeling, Gerhard. *Toward a Theological Theory of Language*. Minneapolis: Fortress Press, 1973.

Frazee, Randy, and Max Lucado, eds. *The Story: The Bible as One Continuing Story of God and His People*. Grand Rapids: Zondervan, 2011.

Wuthnow, Robert. *After Heaven: Spirituality in America Since the 1950s*. Berkeley: University of California Press, 1998.